CW00503214

'Helen offers beautiful biblic
consider our behaviour towa
praying, "Lord, please use t
narrative of being 'for' one ɛ
the next generation.'"
The Revd Anne Calver, Assoᴄᴵᴀᴛᴇ ᴍᴵɴᴵꜱᴛᴇʀ, ꜱᴛᴀɴᴍore Baptist
Church, and Spring Harvest Planning Group

'Most women I know have stumbled into the hurdles of jealousy
and comparison, and it hurts us and sours our relationships. A lot.
Helen's timely book inspires and helps us to navigate a different
path. Read it and walk in freedom!'
Debra Green OBE, Founder and Director, Redeeming Our
Communities

'*The Comparison Trap* is a timely book written to speak directly
to the needs and desires of today's generation, with their cultural
norms of comparison. Helen embodies the very word "passion" as
she writes out of a deep well that is both practical and profoundly
wise. Within this book, readers will feel safe in recognizing their
own competitive nature, as well as having the opportunity truly
to examine why this issue has had an impact on their present-day
relationships. It will also allow them to understand more fully
relationships from the past.

Helen is not timid in calling out the deceptive works of the
enemy that affect the relationships women have with one another.
Additionally, she beautifully exemplifies the very essence of the rich
grace and wisdom women were created to carry.'
Stephanie Henderson, Executive Pastor, New Life Church,
Colorado Springs, USA

'*The Comparison Trap* is a timely and important book for those
of us in the Church who want to build up rather than tear down.

Helen has a wonderful way of getting to the heart of issues, and challenging us with warmth and wisdom to consider not only what we think, but why we think it. After reading this book, I am more grateful than ever for my female friendships, but also more committed than ever to seeing women work and live in unity and love. It's time we set ourselves free from the comparison trap. This book will certainly help.'

Cathy Madavan, speaker, writer and author of *Digging for Diamonds* and *Irrepressible*

'How many times at school did you look across the classroom to see that girl, admiring how much prettier, skinnier and taller than you she was? Years later, maybe you're an adult who every Sunday is glancing through a crowded church at other women who, in your opinion, are so much better than you.

There's something about us girls that makes us want to make comparisons with – rather than celebrate – other women. I don't know why we do it. Perhaps it flows out of our own insecurities. Maybe it's because of the inner jealousies we all battle.

So what's the answer?

My friend Helen beautifully and bravely tackles this difficult subject.

This book will enable you to reflect on how we respond to other women around us, focusing on the comparison and jealousy trap we all face. Helen puts it beautifully when she says, "Christ's truth will tell us what we need to know about the Father, ourselves and other women. In his truth there will be no need to compare negatively or be jealous."

Helen hasn't just written about this concept, but I've watched her live it too. An incredible leader, wife and mother, Helen encourages me to find freedom from negative thoughts and unhealthy comparisons.

I hope that, as you read this book, you will run for Christ,

knowing that he has so much more in store for you when you take your eyes off others and fix them on him.'
Becky Murray, Founder and Director, One By One, <www.oneby one.net>

'*The Comparison Trap* is packed full of insight, wisdom and practical steps to help women be free from the stress and strife of competition. Using the word of God, lots of honest anecdotes and a great deal of revealing research, Helen navigates readers away from the pain of jealousy and into a joy-filled, generous approach to life. If you often compare yourself with the people around you (which applies to very many people), this book is for you.'
Jo Naughton, Co-Lead Pastor, Harvest Church London, and Founder of Healed for Life

'Helen brings the word of God to life, offering incredible insight on the struggles that plague women when comparing themselves with one another. I love Helen's sheer honesty and willingness to share her own journey. *The Comparison Trap* inspires strength and courage in women to overcome their fears of never being good enough. You will certainly be encouraged to remain secure in who you are!'
Nikki Rucci, Senior Pastor, Rivercity Family Church, Brisbane, Australia

'*The Comparison Trap* is a refreshing look at an age-old problem. In this book, Helen calls women to something higher. In a real and honest way, she shines a light into the darkness of what can limit us as women. We are living in a time where the war between women is raging like never before. This means that, as women, we need to put aside all that confines us and band together for the higher mission.'
Letitia Shelton, CEO, City Women, Toowoomba, Australia

'For so many women, the impact of comparison with others is both dramatic and damaging to their own sense of worth and their relationships with others. Helen's insightful and down-to-earth treatment of the subject casts light on the problem and points us to the freedom that is to be found in the love of the Father who made us each unique. It offers a doorway to living "incomparably free".'
Esther Storey, Senior Pastor, CLM Church, Coventry, UK

'I love how Helen is able to present a model of healthy relationships among women, devoid of jealousy and comparison. Once you read this book, you will never be satisfied with anything less. If you desire to reach new levels in relationships, I reckon this book is just for you!'
Marta Tothova, Co-Lead Pastor, Kristus Mestu, Nitra Slovakia and Equippers Church, Budapest, Hungary

Helen is an inspirational author, speaker and leader who was healed from cancer in 1999. Her life is now invested in encouraging people to grow in spiritual maturity and joy-filled trust in the God who brings lasting freedom.

She and her husband Tim serve as Senior Leaders of Wellspring Church (Watford) and enjoy a growing ministry in the wider community and other nations. Married in 1994, Helen and Tim have three children and have lived in the Watford area ever since.

Follow her on Twitter: @HelenRoberts_1.

THE COMPARISON TRAP

Helen Roberts

First published in Great Britain in 2020

Society for Promoting Christian Knowledge
36 Causton Street
London SW1P 4ST
www.spck.org.uk

British Library Cataloguing-in-Publication Data
A catalogue record for this book is available from the British Library

ISBN 978-0-281-08335-0
eBook ISBN 978-0-281-08336-7

Typeset by Falcon Oast Graphic Art Ltd
First printed in Great Britain by Jellyfish Print Solutions
Subsequently digitally printed in Great Britain

eBook by Falcon Oast Graphic Art Ltd

Produced on paper from sustainable forests

Dedicated to my two favourite girls,
Bethany and Hannah:
May you both live your lives incomparably *you*,
joyfully liberated by the love of the Lord,
free from the trappings of comparison.
I am cheering you on all the way.

Contents

Part 4
BODY PERFECT

Part 5
CREATED TO CHAMPION

Acknowledgements

A book is a team effort and this is no exception. I am so grateful for the so many who have made this book possible.

First, my Tim: thank you for letting me camp out longer than normal in my 'writing space' and cheering me on through this project. Thank you for the notes you've left me to discover in my car, by the kettle and on my laptop. Your words have spurred me on and kept the vision in mind. I love you.

For my three favourites: Bethany, thank you for some great conversations along the way and for sharing some of your studies and your perspectives. Thank you for letting me read your essays at just the right time. Even if none of the book titles we came up with that time made the cut, it was so much fun thinking of them with you. Hannah, you have been the most wonderful study-buddy. I have loved that, for so many weeks, we've shared the same space and been able to cheer one another on. You have inspired and championed me and I'm so grateful for this season we've shared. David, you are one of the most encouraging people I know and I love that you have believed in this book and spurred me on not to give up. You teach me so much about gratitude by the attitude you keep. Thank you.

To my sister Carol: thank you for being you and letting me be me. I am so grateful that when it mattered the most you loved Jesus more than you loved me, and because of this you put up with me and loved me more. I am so grateful that you are my sister and that I can know you as a friend.

Brett Jordan: thank you for your love, friendship, perseverance and honesty as you took hold of this manuscript (more than once) with a pen, scissors and scalpel! I am so grateful for you.

Acknowledgements

Cathy Davenport: thank you for sharing the journey and the adventure again! Thank you for your willingness to go out of your comfort zone and not just proofread (that is challenge enough) but invest even more in helping me stay on track.

Stephanie Embree: thank you for being you! I am so grateful for your fearless honesty to say what I needed to hear. Thank you that you never held back from encouraging me or challenging me to cut stuff out or go deeper still. I love your love for books, theology, people and especially for God. I am so grateful he connected us and we get to champion one another for his glory.

Wellspring Church, leadership and staff team: thank you for supporting and encouraging me to keep writing along with all the other things I get to do. Thank you for releasing me into the gift of a sabbatical just at the right time. Thank you for being the most amazing family.

Tony Collins: what an exciting day that was to get a call from an 'Editor at Large'. I will never forget our first meeting and your courage to believe in me and this book. I am so grateful for you, your wisdom and your encouragement.

To all the team at SPCK: thank you for all those who have worked on this book, and the many other books you've published that help and feed so many. Thank you for the hours you've spent in your area of skill to bring this book through to completion. I'm so grateful for the privilege of joining your amazing list of authors.

Introduction

I know none of us sets out to be jealous. None of us intentionally fans jealousy into flame and feeds the hungry green-eyed monster. Yet jealousy is rampant. Of course, jealousy doesn't respect gender and is not caused by the XX chromosome pair, but comparison and jealousy affect many women.

Comparison cripples girls. Comparison causes depression, anxiety and emotional disorders to increase, relationships to break down, insecurities to rise and trust to decrease. Comparison has the power to hold us back, lock us in and hamstring our futures. It's time we were set free from the comparison trap.

There is a narrative that sets women up to fail. Together, we can change this. We can write a new story.

I was at the gym a few months ago and found myself working out near another woman and her personal trainer. She was talking loudly in between her reps, ranting that 'women are simply horrible to women!' I was so saddened by her observation, but somehow not surprised.

A few weeks later I sat in a meeting with some of my charity director colleagues, reflecting on a particularly difficult personnel situation we were dealing with. Someone commented, 'Let's face it, many women don't like to be managed by a woman!' Aargh – this can't be true. I became defensive, yet around the table men and women began agreeing with this observation. Do women really not work well for female bosses? Do female bosses behave worse towards their female subordinates?

This was sadly not a new revelation. It came on top of many years of frustrations. When my husband and I took over the leadership of our church in 1998, we were young and inexperienced in comparison to the four seasoned travellers who had gone before us. We sat for hours in a handover meeting picking their brains and trying to absorb their wisdom. Years on, I couldn't tell you the specifics of all that was handed to us. However, there was a piece of advice that shocked me then – and to be honest I considered it was wrong. But it was stark and memorable. Sadly, time has added personal experience to the advice.

One of the female leaders strongly advised me not to make any *best friends* among women in our church. She said it would cause division and jealousy among the other women if I did. Of course, she advised me to make friends – but not ever to allow best friendships to develop and to avoid being exclusive or over-personal with any woman because other women would become jealous. Friendship could, in her view, create more trouble than it was worth!

I didn't like the advice or even understand it. However, I've come to realize that there are nuggets of truth in her advice. Women have an incredible capacity to compare themselves to other women and as a result get caught in the grip of jealousy, which can move among them in a powerful and destructive way. But the good news is it doesn't have to be this way.

This book will take us on a journey to look at an age-old challenge when jealousy between women can undermine everything we hold dear. We will travel back in time to the fore-parents of faith and see how they battled with comparisons which influenced so much trouble. From Old Testament to New Testament and through to current times, we are going to expose the enemy's strategies which cause us to war against each other, in order that we can understand, oppose and destroy them and, as sisters, advance into the victory Christ has prepared for us.

The battles women faced in biblical times often seem centred on their wombs, but our comparisons are not limited to our physical fertility. Our extended families, communities and especially our workplaces can become the battleground of comparison.

I believe I have received an invitation from the Holy Spirit to urge women to take a fresh stand together and end the battles held against each other, as well as the inner battles we face alone, so that the purposes and glory of the Lord can be realized. It's time to discover a new freedom and begin living life to the full.

As we journey through this together, we're going to look at some of the foundational challenges we all face in our identity and relationships. We're going to look at the impact of women's relationships in the workplace. We're also going to look at some of the inner battles we face and how to discover our uniqueness, being body-fit, before enjoying the freedom that will come when we learn to break free from the comparison trap and become women who champion other women.

I've written this book for women but I also know that men are part of the solution. We can all work together to change the narrative. So if you are courageous enough to pick up this book and come on this journey with us, then I thank you!

To any brave boys willing to get hold of this book and read it – I salute and honour you. May you not only grow into the men you are created and intended to be, but may you champion the women in your world to grow into the women they are created and intended to be!

To men and women in leadership – I hope this book will help you grow as a leader equipped to champion those women around you to thrive. There is a new narrative that we can write together that will enable women to succeed.

To every woman reading this – I am praying for you as I write, in all your uniqueness. May you discover the real you and learn to love who you are. May you conquer comparison with other women and unleash the power of championing women. As you embrace your own freedom from jealousy, you will discover what it truly means to champion other women. I am praying especially that you come to know your Heavenly Father, who has created you for a destiny that requires your involvement. You are loved. You belong. There is so much more for you.

Helen

NB: Bible references are from the New Living Translation unless otherwise stated.

Part 1

TOO CLOSE
TO HOME

1

What kind of woman?

'I really don't want to go to a women's day event,' I moaned. 'Why would I want to spend a whole day with just women?' This wasn't an orientation or attraction issue – just me trying to get out of attending our church's Ladies' Day – about 23 years ago! It wasn't that I didn't like women or preferred the company of men, but the thought of being with *just* women filled me with dread. It seemed like the perfect environment to be misunderstood or judged, or to somehow offend someone.

Rumour has it that women can't get on with each other! Is this a myth or based on fact? There is a popular opinion that women are prone to fall out with other women. Unless we're in someone's inner circle, as the BFF (best friends for ever), then apparently we are lining up, claws outstretched, ready to fight and brawl at the first opportunity – allegedly!

For the record, I was never convinced that the rumour had any merit. My conviction was that personality, rather than gender, produced relationship challenges. I've always been more concerned with championing the message of equality between *genders* to be sidetracked with the relationship between *women*.

But then something happened! I didn't have a blinding-light revelation – nor did I suffer from a major incident where any particular woman declared war on me. Rather, I kept overhearing various conversations, stumbled across a significant number of articles and experienced a few random incidents until I had gained more of a 360-degree perspective. The realization dawned on me that things between women are not as they could be. I sensed God had a better plan for women. The Lord was inviting me to understand what was going on around me, as well as inside me, and to prepare for a transformation into new thinking – a revolution in my heart. The apostle Paul said to the Romans,

> Don't copy the behaviour and customs of this world, but let God transform you into a new person by changing the way you think. Then you will learn to know God's will for you, which is good and pleasing and perfect.
> (Romans 12.2)

The Father has a good, pleasing and perfect will for all his children, and right now there is a conversation for his daughters that you are invited to join. It's a conversation that could be transformational!

Are there perhaps some behaviours and customs of our world that we are in danger of copying when we could be living a transformed life?

Many relationships between women are amazing, life-enhancing and wonderful. I have some incredible female friends who share life with me. These are friendships that have spanned many years, some many decades. I've also had the privilege of observing other women in their friendship circles and can see the times when female friendship is simply brilliant. Sometimes the relationship challenges are not with the ones in our immediate friendship circle but are in the wider context that we live in – women in our communities, our workplace, our professional sphere, our extended family or, often via social media, on a global platform.

There are factors in the behaviour and customs of our world that seem to have become the enemy of women's relationships and emotional well-being, and we're going to explore these and the negative effects they can have: in particular, competition and comparison, which can lead to jealousy. Even if our relationships appear healthy there are too many women suffering from the fallout of the negative effects of comparison.

In an article for *The New York Times*, US writer and producer Emily Gordon declared, 'Women compete, compare, undermine and undercut one another – at least that is the prevailing notion of how we interact.'[1] Is this reputation deserved? Or are we being set up, by some conspiracy theory, to feud?

How are we to negotiate our way through the minefield narrative? Is the reputation deserved? Are we trapped by comparison and jealousy and is there a way to escape?

According to Gordon there are

theories of why women are competitive in indirectly aggressive ways. Evolutionary psychology, which uses natural selection to explain our modern behaviours, says that women need to protect themselves (read: their wombs) from physical harm so indirect aggression keeps us safe while lowering the stock of other women.

Yikes! – my word – as Gordon continues, quoting psychology professor Noam Shpancer's words from *Psychology Today*,

'As women come to consider being prized by men their ultimate source of strength, worth, achievement and identity, they are compelled to battle other women for the prize.' In short: When our value is tied to the people who can impregnate us, we turn on each other.[2]

Are women competing with one another in order to be 'impregnated' by whoever appears to hold the prize which we desire? Are the prizes too few and far between, so that there are not enough for us all?

Sport is surely a place where competition is expected and celebrated. But in 2019 South African Caster Semenya lost her discrimination case against the International Association of Athletics

Federation (IAAF). 'Semenya, who has won the last 29 of her 800m races, was born with intersex traits – meaning her body produces atypically high levels of testosterone.'[3] She is naturally both fast and strong. If Semenya was going to be permitted to run in these shorter races then it was ruled she would have to take medication to reduce her natural testosterone levels. Clothing manufacturer Nike used Semenya in one of their promotional campaigns, where she is heard to ask,

> Would it be easier for you if I wasn't so fast? Would it be simpler if I stopped winning? Would you be more comfortable if I was less proud? Would you prefer I hadn't worked so hard? Or just didn't run? Or chose a different sport? Or stopped at my first steps? That's too bad – because I was born to do this![4]

In track and field the IAFF's goal was to have a level playing field. It was seen to be an unfair advantage for Semenya to have more testosterone than the average female athlete. But is it fairer that Semenya has to medicate against who she naturally is in order that she should be less distinct and become more like some of the other athletes?

If competing as women in sport can become this complicated, it is hardly surprising it can be a challenge in other spheres too. In whatever lane we are running, competition and comparison between women cause problems because – we are all different! The diversity of womanhood is huge. From personality to preferences, aptitudes and abilities, from IQ to EQ and from features to feelings – we are all different. Womanhood is a vast spectrum.

When I was younger I always felt too tall and too fat. Being big in height I felt big in every way. I grew tall more quickly than my teen peers and had to wait several years before some caught up. If being more like other girls and what I interpreted as a 'girlie-girl' was a goal, then it was not something I felt I could reach. And as for the variety in body hair – that's a whole other challenge. I've often wondered what luxury item I would choose on *Desert Island Discs*. Had the Bible not been standard issue then I would be torn, feeling that I should take it, but honestly I would probably opt for tweezers!

Looking back on photos from my teenage years, I can see that my feelings were not totally reliable. I was taller than most of my peers and even my 'big' sister; however, my developing body was, for the most part, adequately proportioned – just tall. Body dysmorphia can cause us to focus on what we see as our flaws and even imaginary imperfections, and can lead to significant social and mental challenges. When we are uncomfortable about ourselves then we are more likely to be drawn into comparisons with other women.

American gymnast Katelyn Ohashi discussed her challenge with her body image, saying,

> because the body is such an obviously integral part of sport, it's vital that it is regarded positively. Subconsciously, if we're thinking negatively about it, we're much less likely to look after it properly. In sport, that's disastrous . . . everybody's bodies are different and there's not a single body that is the perfect body because there are constant trends. Being comfortable with the only person that matters, yourself, is something that you can for ever work towards. You're the only person that has your back and you're the only person that has your skin 100 per cent of the time.[5]

She's right! Body-beauty has been interpreted differently over the years. With ever-changing trends around us and the changing tides of emotions within us, we have to navigate our way through the minefield of diversity that is womanhood. This challenge becomes even more complicated when we compare ourselves with other women.

When wanting to avoid the company of women at *that* ladies' day I realize I felt more comfortable, perhaps even safer, if there was a bunch of guys around me rather than a bunch of girls. There seemed to be a complexity in the company of a large gathering of women that, as a younger woman, I did not feel skilled or qualified to navigate. Avoidance seemed easier.

Rolling the clock forward, I find myself smiling at how the Lord has allowed me to lead women's events and speak at many women's conferences. A gathering of women that once would have terrified me now inspires me – and I've grown to realize how a roomful of women can change the world! More of that later.

So let's talk about you for a minute. If you were to describe yourself in a few words, what would you say? You *might* start by describing your looks, but there is so much more to you than that. Describe your emotional well-being today; what about your dreams – the ones you have now and the ones from your past – how would you describe them? Could you find words to articulate your strengths and successes as well as your failures?

When you describe yourself, what measure do you use? I mean, are you comparing yourself against a former version or a future vision of yourself – or are you comparing yourself to someone else, fictional or real? Do you carry regrets from choices you've made or are you at peace with where, and who, you are?

I know we're getting personal straight away – but as we continue our conversation we're going to be looking at the narrative of womanhood that surrounds us, and it's helpful to stop and listen to the private story that is within you. To go on any journey you first have to know where you are starting from. This is our starting evaluation – how are you doing, right now?

2

The narrative

One of the customs in our culture is trading on reputations. What begins as simply playground antics, as girls whisper into each other's ears, progresses into chat rooms, gets snapped on a chat stream and can become normalized as a behavioural pattern all too easily. In the quest to be liked, accepted or promoted in our social spheres, gossip will often elevate someone at the expense of another. This is not limited to the trials of teenage girls. It would seem that this behaviour is often honed in the masterclass of womanhood.

In a report produced by Florida State University's Department of Psychology, Tania Reynolds, a doctoral student, studied adult women's use of gossiping techniques as adopted by teenage girls to damage another woman's reputation:

> It's consequential because a woman's reputation still predicts her access to romantic partners, friendships or professional collaborations, and this research shows gossip can substantially shift social perceptions. People tend to give more weight to negative personal information because they consider it a truer indication of a person's character than positive details.[1]

If we're brutally honest with ourselves, I'm sure we'll admit we've all succumbed at some stage to the temptation of passing on gossip deliberately or inadvertently, even if we've perhaps wrapped it up in the packaging of 'sharing a concern' or, worse, a prayer need! Is the motivation behind gossip really to destroy another female's reputation in order to enhance our own future – whether that be with regard to fertility, promotion or our own reputation? We might also have realized that we've sometimes become the subject of someone else's gossip.

Are women trying to construct a narrative around themselves that helps them progress, even at the expense of another woman? Do women talk about other women to deflate the reputation of their subject for their own self-promotion?

We have a seemingly insatiable appetite to read about the private lives of celebrities, royals and various 'people of interest'. Column after column is written and we absorb them, often without corroboration: stories that seduce us into thinking that we actually know the people themselves, convincing ourselves we are friends.

For former First Lady of the United States of America Michelle Obama, being the subject of media interest was her regular experience. Journalists fought for their own reputation by getting their articles published. She began to witness how her life became expounded by people who didn't take the time to know her personally but rather used her reputation to build their own. The newsreels are not produced solely by women; however, Michelle Obama felt a particular impact when a female journalist added to the cacophony. In her book *Becoming*, Michelle Obama admitted, 'I found it odd and sad that such a harsh critique would come from another professional woman, someone who had not bothered to get to know me but was now trying to shape my story in a cynical way.'[2]

As few of us will have the opportunity to become personal friends with Michelle Obama, the opinion most of us hold about her will be shaped predominantly by the media. A diet of gossip, though, will surely help produce a lifestyle of gossip. Before we can break free from the comparison trap and tackle the jealousy between women, we need to look at the narrative we are buying into.

I'm going to be completely honest with you – I've recently had one of those parent-fail experiences that was an all-new low for me! This is a terrible confession, but in the process between my research and writing I managed to give my kids food poisoning! Clearly that is a parent-fail – but, if it helps, I didn't do it deliberately! By means of explanation (but not an excuse) I was trying to get back into my writing space and those unidentifiable burgers at the back of the freezer seemed like an easy meal choice. Had I known that this diet-of-convenience would produce some synchronized midnight vomiting for two of our kids I would certainly have taken more notice of the use-by date!

What we feed our kids will have an effect, one way or another. Very few people would intentionally give their kids food poisoning, but are we as careful with some of the influences we unintentionally feed them? There is a narrative that many of us are feeding our young children which is fuelling comparison and jealousy between women.

Have you ever paused to consider why so many of the fairy-tale stories we feed our kids fuel the notion that women can't get on with women? Cinderella is trapped by the abuse of her ugly stepsisters and wicked stepmother. Rapunzel is locked up in the tower by the wicked witch. Snow White is left for dead by her wicked stepmother. The only positive female role models are the make-believe fairy godmothers, who don't actually exist. Okay, so I appreciate none of them exist and they are all fairy tales. But the point is: we are inadvertently feeding our young girls a message that the women in their world are against them.

Of course, there are some other stories where women learn to value their relationship with each other, and so perhaps I had better let it go, but at the risk of sounding like a frozen record (did you see what I did there?) our children can be drip-fed a diet of stories pitting women against women. So as girls and boys grow up, this narrative is normalized.

I'm not saying that our young girls should never watch or read these fairy tales, but surely we need to provide a balanced diet for our girls to grow up healthy and confident.

Feuding females are not merely a topic for childhood stories. I came across a surprising war between two women which became both a book and a musical, called *War Paint*. Our entertainment is made of competing, jealous women – and we buy it. This particular story, though, is based on a true situation with no fairy godmother in sight to save the day.

Two leading women from the cosmetic industry were, apparently, at distinct odds with one another. In her book *War Paint*, Lindy Woodhead said,

> Whilst Helena Rubenstein had several rivals in collecting African art, in the beauty business she had only one. The two of them competed to see who could acquire the most accolades and the most profit. Neither could bear to say her rival's name out loud. To Helena Rubenstein, her competitor was always 'the other one'. To her rival, Helena Rubenstein was always 'that woman'. Between them, these formidable women created the luxury beauty business as it is known today. The 'other one's' name was . . . Elizabeth Arden.[3]

To be friendly rivals and business competitors is one thing, but to be side-stepping and snubbing formidable foes to the extent that the enemy's name cannot be spoken is going to extremes. Silent treatment, 'unfriending' and blocking of another can often be weapons employed in an assault of revenge. To refuse to utter a person's name is to hold her in such contempt that a war is fuelled rather than peace declared.

The competition between these two women damaged relationships with other women, limited their friendship circles and had an impact on their family relationships too (Rubenstein even employed Arden's ex-husband in a bid to score a point and stay ahead). Most noticeable, perhaps, was that their feuding relationship became their focus, draining their energy to such a degree that it had an effect on their business success.

Woodhead wrote:

> Had the two women spent less time bickering they might have had their antennae more finely tuned to a far greater threat to their virtual stranglehold over the market in America . . . Miss Arden and Madame [Rubenstein] should have been preparing to do battle with Revlon, but they were still too busy fighting each other. They would come to regret it.[4]

This was not a healthy rivalry. The toxicity of jealous competition had the power to divert these feuding women's focus and dampen their success.

These intelligent, articulate, entrepreneurial women were arch-enemies. They never met face to face, yet managed to keep the feud burning remotely. Their reputations and rivalry are remembered and captured in the book and on Broadway, for our entertainment. Apparently these founding leaders of the twentieth-century beauty business agreed on only one thing, and that was in 'the quest for beautiful skin – cleanse away grime, exfoliate dead cells, moisturise and keep out of the sun'.[5]

The celebrity culture regularly preys on our fascination for delving into the private lives of famous females. In a 'real-life' fairy tale, our popular media scrutinizes the relationship between two modern-day princesses and fuels the narrative of a feud. Kate Middleton is portrayed as the perfect princess, whereas Meghan Markle is portrayed as the wicked stepsister.

University media and communications professor and gender commentator Professor Catherine Lumby is reported to have identified that

> there is a theme at play: It is completely gendered. She [the duchess] is a 'second' princess, so she's got to be cast as somehow the evil or the bad princess, as part of a contest between

her and Kate Middleton. It is a fairy tale basically, built into deep psychological and literary stereotypes about women being in contest and women who have privilege.[6]

Setting these two women against each other to be feuding females is surely repeating the history of the headlines akin to when Diana, Princess of Wales, was pursued relentlessly by the paparazzi. In an open letter to support *Hello!* magazine's social media #helloto kindness campaign, Sarah Ferguson, Duchess of York, wrote:

Women, in particular, are constantly pitted against and com-pared with each other in a way that reminds me of how people tried to portray Diana and me all the time as rivals, which is something neither of us ever really felt.[7]

If they were never enemies, why was this the storyline of choice? Why must there be a wicked princess threatening the popular princess?

Businesswomen, members of the royal family and A-listers from the pop world are all subject to public battles between women. Rivalries sensationalized with songs, memes and gossip provide fuel for the fire.

When did choosing to 'unfollow' someone on Twitter become a newsworthy action? In a well-documented feud between Taylor Swift and Katy Perry, every follow, unfollow, song lyric and Instagram montage fed their audience's hunger, while still leaving them hungry for more. Every interview these artists did over a number of years eventually included questioning about their relationship rivalry. How wearisome it must have been when a disagreement with another woman was all everyone else wanted to talk about.

It was all said to have begun when some dancers from Perry's 'world' joined Swift for a season, only to express the desire to jump ship in time for a fresh tour with Katy Perry. Surely in the world of music and entertainment there are many dancers and musicians who appear in multiple contexts. However, this was not simply left as 'business' for long, because it became public and personal. Whether it was Taylor personally or her team, the dancers were swiftly sacked and became 'available' to join Katy. It was a beef that caused 'bad blood' and had an impact on her 'reputation' (as the song titles revealed).

If we feed our daughters, and ourselves, with a diet of feuding females, it's no wonder that women are set up to fail. If we constantly want to find a wicked woman near every great one, then battle lines are drawn. Weapons are loaded.

3

Sisters at war

Battles between biblical women seem most often to have been centred on their wombs! Women would have womb-wars against each other, or a private battle on their own, linked again to their ability to reproduce. Children gave a woman the reputation of being favoured by God as well as securing her financial future.

What we have the potential to produce from our lives can become a source of competition and jealousy towards others. We can literally breed jealousy.

Genesis tells the story of two young sisters who were both married to the same man within a week of each other. Over many years, as their story unfolds, the fertility-centric competition between the sisters grows: a private womb-war that eventually had an impact on their wider community and the next generation in significant ways. Wars between women rarely stay private for long.

Leah and Rachel were the daughters of Laban and nieces to Aunt Rebekah and Uncle Isaac. When Jacob met Rachel at the feeding well he was fleeing his brother Esau's anger and his father's disappointment, to the relative safety of the estate of his mother's brother, Uncle Laban. Within a month of being there, having proved himself useful at handling livestock, Jacob negotiated a price to marry Rachel.

The writer of Genesis describes the difference between the sisters, saying, 'There was no sparkle in Leah's eyes, but Rachel had a beautiful figure and a lovely face' (Genesis 29.17). The lack of sparkle could be understood as a lack of facial beauty, or perhaps referred to poor vision, even blindness. Either way, it is clear – Rachel was recognized as beautiful and Leah was not!

Jacob's love for Rachel was so strong that he was willing to work for seven years before he married her. However, to secure his elder daughter's marriage Laban tricked Jacob into marrying her first. So Jacob had to renegotiate marrying Rachel, having been tricked into the wrong partnership with Leah. A week after Jacob had married his first bride, Laban permitted Rachel to marry him also. While those seven days might have felt like the longest ever experienced, the previous seven years had felt so brief: 'his love for her was so strong that it seemed to him but a few days' (Genesis 29.20).

How hard it must have been for Leah to be the older sister with no one wanting to marry her. In a culture where marriage and maternity were essential for a woman to survive, she was not chosen. The only way her father was able to secure her marriage, and her future, was to trick Jacob into marrying her, with the use of veils and perhaps some wine, the cunning support of servant Zilpah and, of course, the dim lamplight that wouldn't reveal detail in the shadows of the tents! It wasn't just Leah who had dull eyes that night – Jacob had no clue until it dawned on him at dawn! It wouldn't have been a hard trick to pull off, but all the time that the marriage was being consummated Leah would have known he wasn't loving her. He might have been close to her, intimate with her, but in his mind she was someone else!

In the midst of their story, Father God's compassion is on display. 'When the LORD saw that Leah was unloved, he enabled her to have children, but Rachel could not conceive' (Genesis 29.31). Despite the absence of human love, there was never an absence of the Heavenly Father's love.

Even with all that was in her favour, Rachel was not content. 'When Rachel saw that she wasn't having any children for Jacob, she became jealous of her sister. She pleaded with Jacob, "Give me children, or I'll die!"' (Genesis 30.1).

As Israeli writer Liora Ravid notes,

> each lacked something that her sister had, and that something embittered her life . . . Undoubtedly, the spurned Leah longed for some of the love her husband lavished on her sister. She had good reason to envy the beautiful, beloved Rachel – and the opposite is even more true. Hated as she was, Leah bore many children, so her position in Jacob's home was firm.[1]

How often do we lose sight of what we have and instead notice what someone else has? Even in our home life, school life and work life, our eyes can be drawn to see the thing that someone else has that we don't. Comparison can produce discontentment and jealousy.

Rachel, beautiful, chosen and beloved – the one who had so much – became so consumed by jealousy for her sister that she hatched a plan and decided that if her womb was closed she would claim the womb of her servant, Bilhah, as her own. The writer of Genesis explains the meaning of the names of her first two sons, Dan and Naphtali, through this surrogate arrangement and these names reveal the battle in which Rachel feels involved.

> Bilhah became pregnant and presented him with a son. Rachel named him Dan, for she said, 'God has vindicated me! He has heard my request and given me a son.' Then Bilhah became pregnant again and gave Jacob a second son. Rachel named him Naphtali, for she said, 'I have struggled hard with my sister, and I'm winning!'
> (Genesis 30.5–8)

She was *winning* against her *sister*! Rachel's identity, worth and future had become entangled with winning this womb-war over her sister. The struggle between the women was very real. Rachel did go on to personally conceive and over time delivered two babies, Joseph and Benjamin – but at such a cost!

Ravid explains:

> Birth order played an especially important role when a man had several senior wives. The senior wife who bore his first-born son – the future heir who would become head of the family – was superior to the other senior wives. Still, the status of the heir's mother was vulnerable . . . since Leah was married in exchange for Rachel's bride-price, she had the status of senior wife, and thus all six of her sons were higher in rank than Joseph and Benjamin.[2]

As Leah and Rachel's battle went on unchecked, the jealousy between them kept being reborn alongside the babies. Perhaps the greatest tragedy of their story is that Rachel never escaped the comparison trap. Not satisfied with providing Joseph with three children, either through Bilhah or through giving birth herself, she wanted more. Tragically, in childbirth with her second son, Benjamin, she died.

Oh, the sadness in this story! Having begged her husband for children, saying without them she would die, Rachel had the children and died in childbirth. Such a tragedy. This beautiful young woman never found contentment. She had been so loved – but it was never enough. The unquenchable desire to give birth to life cost her very life. Jealousy will always prevent you from living life to the full.

Leah and Rachel's jealousy even carried on into the next generation, as all the sons of Leah were consumed with jealousy for Joseph, the first biological son born to Rachel. Such is the legacy of jealousy.

Remember *that* ladies' day I mentioned in Chapter 1? All attempts to avoid it failed and I found myself attending (somewhat reluctantly). Between sessions I had a brief corridor conversation with one of the speakers, a prophetic leader, during which I heard myself confessing that Tim and I were trying to conceive but I was not convinced that my womb was 'fit for purpose'. The reason for my concern was that I had both endometriosis and polycystic ovaries. The prophetic leading lady was not accepting my negative confession, and without so much as an 'our Father' started praying against the 'spirit of barrenness' over my life. I found myself weeping – accompanied by a loud wailing. A deep, hidden, inner pain was revealed with the release of tears that enabled me to experience the love and presence of my Heavenly Father's embrace in a fresh way. I felt loved, listened to, noticed by the Lord in ways that I hadn't previously. This was not a moment of angelic visitation but of divine timing. Not much more than nine months after this, our first daughter let out her first cry!

Perhaps I should have been satisfied, but our first daughter was so gorgeous we wanted another one and we simply didn't feel 'complete' as a family! I assumed that, now I had had one child, my previous gynaecological challenges were over. However, my womb missed the minutes of that meeting and was not choosing to comply. Secondary infertility introduced itself to me. It was nearly five years before my womb became home to life again, five years of month-after-month tests and tears. I was painfully reminded my dream was still *just* a dream. I would walk around our town and it would seem as if *everyone* else was pregnant. We did our part, the doctors did their part with medication, scopes and even drills, but life didn't miraculously appear. I felt like a failure. I couldn't conceive. However, while I didn't begin to carry a baby within me I did begin to carry something else – jealousy!

Sometimes we can wrongly see everyone else as enjoying what we would like to have. We 'see' how *everyone* is dating, or all our friends are married or getting a promotion or buying a home.

Jealousy is a weird thing! To save me from sugar-coating it, let's say it as it is! Jealousy is a sin. It's a heart condition in which we feel entitled to something, or someone, that we don't have. As the Ten

Commandments specified, no one is to 'set your heart on anything that is your neighbour's' (Exodus 20.17, *The Message*). It's a state of mind when we think we have been wronged and we focus on what we *don't* have, as if somebody else has something that is actually ours. Jealousy suggests that something has been stolen from us and we are justified in wanting it back! Jealousy can appear in any sphere of our life if we don't guard against it.

Furthermore, jealousy will eventually spill over and affect our relationships on a number of levels, threatening to destroy much that we hold dear.

As we post our finest, carefully angled Instagram shot, we present a life to be 'liked' by others. We scroll through our feeds and ingest images as carefully crafted as our own, yet seeing others' images as real – and we want what they've got. We compare ourselves, critique others and, let's be honest, compete. Comparison is the on-ramp to the road marked 'jealousy', which can fuel competition between women, yet this is not a new challenge simply triggered by social media.

Back to 2001. After years of monthly disappointment, I was walking around the shopping centre in our town, utterly convinced that everyone was pregnant. Everyone except me! There was so much that I could have been thanking God for as I walked around the shops. I could have thanked him for my salvation, that I was loved so wholeheartedly by my Heavenly Father. I could have thanked him for the love of my best friend and husband (they are one and the same person!). He's amazing. Why wasn't I giving thanks for him on this day? Gosh, there were many years when I'd focused on requesting the Lord to end my years of singleness. Why was I not holding on to contentment and gratitude just for that? I could have been grateful for our beautiful daughter, who was in school at that very moment, learning, laughing, thriving. I could have been giving thanks that I was still alive. I'd been on the receiving end of a significant and miraculous healing from secondary, terminal cancer!

Why was I not constantly grateful and simply satisfied? We led our church, had purpose in life. We lived in a house! We had a car to drive. Surely there was something that I could have been grateful for. Anything! Yet on this day I walked around the shopping centre and I felt overlooked and abandoned. Why were my prayers falling on deaf ears? Why was silence the only answer I was getting to the repeated prayer for a child? Why could I not conceive again? Why was everyone else on the planet pregnant except me?

This was not just a one-day experience. It was becoming the definition of a season! The writer of Proverbs was right: 'unrelenting disappointment leaves you heartsick' (Proverbs 13.12, *The Message*). Discontentment and longing were growing into weeds of jealousy.

I would like to say that I fell on my knees, confessed, repented and walked away liberated. But that would not be true!

Around that time, I talked to my sister and something was said that I didn't appreciate. I let that fuel the jealousy in my heart. She was pregnant with her *third* child and I didn't stop myself from comparing. It was as if every pregnant person in the world that I'd observed in the shopping centre was projected on to my pregnant sister. Bless her – she had no idea! I decided to write her a letter to explain why what she had said hurt me. I felt she should be enlightened to what was actually going on in my life at the time, as if she had no idea already. But instead I poured the toxicity of my jealous heart on to the pages of the letter and posted a ticking time-bomb of my own sin to her home. If my sister didn't love Jesus more than she loves me that would have been the end of my relationship with her! She didn't get pregnant to hurt me. Her children were not a weapon against me. Yet I'd allowed comparison to fuel a judgement which concluded that I was being wronged!

The reason for my pain was real and my disappointment in my situation was real, yet that did not justify my response. The hurt I was carrying needed to be healed, and so while I needed to talk and reconcile things with my sister I also needed to talk and reconcile with Jesus. The toxicity of my thinking was blocking my relationship with him – that's what sin does!

As I became aware of how I had let my hurt harden my heart and fuel sin, I also became aware that the grace of Jesus was enough for me. Repentance for my wrong attitudes, words and actions led to an acceptance of my situation and released gratitude with fresh revelation that I was, in fact, on the receiving end of Jesus' promise of a 'rich and satisfying life' (John 10.10). I was not *owed* a baby. I was not entitled to have whatever I wanted.

Even though I did eventually have two more children, as far as the Lord was concerned I don't think whether or not I was ever going to have another child was the pressing issue. He is always desiring that we have an intimate and loving relationship with him first. So dealing with the jealousy that I was carrying was far more important. The Lord is always longing for us eagerly to pursue his *presence* more than we pursue his *presents*.

You might never have compared the fruitfulness of your womb with anyone else – but you have probably compared the fruitfulness of your relationships, your studies, your home, your health, your body shape, your hair, your nails, your family or your work. I've compared most of them too! Every time my eyes drift to compare what I don't have in comparison to what others seemingly have, the Lord invites me back to him. Jealousy of others blocks intimacy with him, and he doesn't want anything to come between us.

So maybe, before you read the next page, now would be a good time to have a conversation with the Lord about any comparisons that you are aware you've been making.

4

Cooking up resentment

In order to escape the comparison trap we will need to be honest with ourselves about the decisions we make and the regrets we might carry. It's time to shake them off.

In the New Testament there is another story of two sisters, where the consequences of one sister's choices are the cause of resentment and are projected on to her sister in a relational battle of priorities, much as I projected my jealousy on to my sister and Rachel projected hers on to Leah. This story is about two sisters called Martha and Mary.

> As Jesus and the disciples continued on their way to Jerusalem, they came to a certain village where a woman named Martha welcomed him into her home. Her sister, Mary, sat at the Lord's feet, listening to what he taught. But Martha was distracted by the big dinner she was preparing. She came to Jesus and said, 'Lord, doesn't it seem unfair to you that my sister just sits here while I do all the work? Tell her to come and help me.'
>
> But the Lord said to her, 'My dear Martha, you are worried and upset over all these details! There is only one thing worth being concerned about. Mary has discovered it, and it will not be taken away from her.'
> (Luke 10.38–42)

For a rabbi to have female disciples was not common, and Jesus was affirming that his love and reach extended to women. Mary had discovered a truth of God's grace and mercy. She discovered the truth of salvation. She discovered that the love of the Heavenly Father was extended personally to her. Mary discovered a truth that liberated her from sin's traps. What she had discovered was not going to be taken away from her – by anyone! The Lord was not going to take it away from her and nor was he going to allow the jealous, negative thinking of Martha to interfere with Mary's learning.

In a few words of this story we learn so much about Martha. She is a home-owner and so is relatively wealthy and not a 'kept woman'. She is a decision-maker and decides who comes into her home, and she has chosen Jesus, having clearly recognized he is a significant man.

However, Martha, like many of us, over-extended herself. She wanted to bless her guests but became overburdened in the process. Perhaps in a bid to impress her guests with her fancy cooking, or perhaps because she hadn't realized how many people were in Jesus' party – whatever the reason, preparing the meal was becoming arduous and she was getting stressed, even though this had been her idea in the first place. She was having the equivalent of buyer's remorse!

Have you ever done that? Made a choice and then regretted it when the consequences of that choice differed from what you had imagined? Choosing to study a certain course before realizing it would involve making live presentations in front of your peers, accepting that job before realizing how long the commute was going to take in the rush hour or having a child before realizing you weren't going to get a full night's sleep again – for years! Sometimes the consequences of our decisions become a matter of regret.

Martha loved the idea of a houseful of guests enjoying her food – until she realized that meant kneading the bread, preparing the herbs for the meat and finding the bottle of wine she knew was in the back of the cupboard somewhere but for the life of her couldn't find now! Everything was a good idea – until it became so difficult.

Here was the real challenge. Could Martha have simplified things and let the 'big dinner' be smaller? Or could she have apologized to her guests that the meal would be served a little later than expected so that the timeline was more manageable? Or could she have even asked someone directly for help? Instead, she turned to Jesus as if her sister Mary was in the wrong. She challenged Jesus that Mary was the one with the wrong priorities. Martha tried to manipulate Mary by speaking to Jesus rather than by directly and simply admitting she was out of her depth. Have you ever vented your frustrations about a Mary to someone other than her?

When overwhelmed, rather than owning her own responsibilities she tries to pass them off – via Jesus.

If we want to become women who conquer comparison and stop suffering with jealousy of other women, then we too would do well to work out which of our decisions and responsibilities we can *own*. Then we won't hold others unfairly responsible for our emotional and physical well-being.

Research professor Brené Brown says:

> It is so much easier to cause pain than feel pain and people are taking their pain and they are working it out on other people . . . It's okay if you have got crazy stuff going on – join the club, we all do! Just don't off load your hard stuff on other people.[1]

When our actions feel instigated by Jesus, the consequences often seem more bearable. Yet, when the idea was ours in the first place, regrets can be overwhelming – especially if there is no one to shoulder the burden with us.

Jesus invites us to let him shoulder burdens alongside us, saying:

> Come to me, all of you who are weary and carry heavy burdens, and I will give you rest. Take my yoke upon you. Let me teach you, because I am humble and gentle at heart, and you will find rest for your souls. For my yoke is easy to bear, and the burden I give you is light.
> (Matthew 11.28–30)

So while the challenges might be extensive, his grace and strength are limitless. This farming image referred to the practice of yoking two oxen together. Whenever possible an older ox, bringing wisdom and experience, would be yoked with a younger ox, who brought the strength and energy. The wooden yoke would fit over both their shoulders as they walked side by side, dragging a plough behind them. As they moved forward their individual strengths would provide a deeper, straighter furrow.

Life can be tough. It can be tiring. It is not always like the perfect holiday. There are times when we can wake up feeling as tired as when we went to bed.

There is a 'wisdom' that is often quoted that God won't give you more than you can handle, as if whatever comes our way in life we will be able to cope with. This might make a pretty Instagram post or fridge magnet, but it is not true. What is written, however, assures us that no temptation will be too great for us.

> The temptations in your life are no different from what others experience. And God is faithful. He will not allow the temptation to be more than you can stand. When you are tempted, he will show you a way out so that you can endure.
> (1 Corinthians 10.13)

From Paul's letter to the Corinthians we understand that we are not encouraged to personally handle alone everything in life that comes our way. If we could handle all of life personally, why would we need God? It is in fact the opposite – there will be more in life that we can handle ourselves. But we can take courage because when we are yoked with Jesus things are no longer dependent on what we can handle. As Paul discovered:

> I will boast only about my weaknesses. If I wanted to boast, I would be no fool in doing so, because I would be telling the

truth. But I won't do it, because I don't want anyone to give me credit beyond what they can see in my life or hear in my message, even though I have received such wonderful revelations from God. So to keep me from becoming proud, I was given a thorn in my flesh, a messenger from Satan to torment me and keep me from becoming proud.

Three different times I begged the Lord to take it away. Each time he said, 'My grace is all you need. My power works best in weakness.' So now I am glad to boast about my weaknesses, so that the power of Christ can work through me. That's why I take pleasure in my weaknesses, and in the insults, hardships, persecutions, and troubles that I suffer for Christ. For when I am weak, then I am strong.

(2 Corinthians 12.5–10)

Martha might have wanted to show that she could handle the responsibilities of the meal. She might have been motivated by a desire for Jesus to be blessed. She might have just wanted to bless all of her guests with her hospitality. Her level of stress, however, would suggest she wanted to *impress* her guests. Pressure to impress and prove ourselves in any given context can lead us to be performance-driven and striving for approval. When we are motivated with the desire to *impress* Jesus rather than *bless* him, our burdens will increase.

Cognitive neuroscientist Dr Caroline Leaf says:

One of the main reasons we can experience performance anxiety is due to the fact that we base our identity on a role we play such as athlete or student. Athletes often define their identity on their ability to perform a specific action on the field – every time they go play their sport their identity is in a state of uncertainty, which can make them insecure and anxious about who they are and their self-worth, especially if they do not win. Yet there are a variety of factors involved in winning, and sometimes we just have bad days – this should not affect the way we value our own worth. Nevertheless, in many cases, when we have certain goals or standards that we cannot live up to (whether from ourselves or others), we can feel like a fraud, even though no one can perform perfectly all the time. We are so focused on the goal that we forget to enjoy the process, which makes it difficult for us to change or adjust our expectations.[2]

Remember that, rather than the misconception that God will not allow life to become more than we can handle, what Paul actually said was:

> The temptations in your life are no different from what others experience. And God is faithful. He will not allow the temptation to be more than you can stand. When you are tempted, he will show you a way out so that you can endure.
> (1 Corinthians 10.13)

For every temptation to compare ourselves or become jealous of another woman – Jesus will show us a way out! For every burden to strive to impress others through our performance – Jesus will show us a way out. For every temptation we face to go it alone and do things in our own strength – Jesus will show us a way out. There is no temptation towards comparison, negative competition and jealousy that we will face regarding any woman on the planet where Jesus won't show us a way out. Such is his grace and strength. To conquer comparison we need to discover Jesus' way out!

The more Martha slammed her way around the kitchen, drawing attention to her misery and stress, the more she couldn't see the alternatives. Jesus was right there – in her house – yet she became so entrenched in what she could do *for* him that she missed the opportunity to be *with* him. Then she added the temptation of comparing what her sister was *not* doing and became angrier.

If we measure ourselves by *what we do* for others, even for Jesus, we miss discovering the liberation of *becoming who* Jesus wants us to become. If we compare what we bring to the table, like Martha, with the women in our lives, at work or on our social media platforms, we can become frustrated with jealousy. If we compare ourselves with others we can conclude that we are always the one to initiate the conversations, to send the first text or make the first call. We come to think that it's always us that stays longest in the office or contributes the most in the meeting. Our frustrations too will increase.

Martha's way out of the temptation to foster anger against her sister would have been to stop, sit down and simply *be* with Jesus. If Jesus could rustle up a meal for 5,000 with the meagre ingredients of some loaves and fish, I'm sure he could have done something incredible with what Martha had already prepared and had in her kitchen.

All Martha could see, though, was the food that would not cook itself and the sister who was lounging around doing nothing to help. She didn't realize that the way out was sitting in her house.

Our human brain processes positive and negative experiences differently. Negative thoughts and experiences get ruminated on in more detail as we churn over events and embed them in our memory banks. Positive experiences are enjoyed but are often more fleetingly appreciated. Critical words can be held on to far longer than affirming ones.

When we ruminate on these negative experiences we are creating neuro-pathways in our thinking. It is this negativity bias which can increase the collateral damage in relationships when jealous comparison goes unchecked.

Again, this brain activity might be traced back to the survival instinct of our ancestors that predisposes us to give special attention to anything in our environment that might harm us.

Our brains have a huge capacity, such that 'not only do negative events and experiences imprint more quickly, but they also linger longer than positive ones', according to researcher Dr Randy Larsen.

This stickiness is known as positive–negative asymmetry or the negativity bias. In other words, for a multitude of reasons including biology and chemistry, we're more likely to register an insult or negative event than we are to take in a compliment or recall details of a happy event. The negativity bias can even cause you to dwell on something negative even if something positive is equally or more present. For example, you might spend all day with a friend and have a wonderful time, but if they make one small comment that perturbs you, you may end up remembering the day just for that comment – categorising the experience as negative when the entire day was actually positive.[3]

We will come back to this again, but in the meantime now might be a good time for a personal health check. Remember that 'The temptations in your life are no different from what others experience' (1 Corinthians 10.13), so therefore the propensity to be drawn to criticism and negative thoughts are the same for everyone – and to each of us the Lord assures us that he will provide a way out.

Paul offers the assurance that we can all find a way out from the temptation to wallow in our own misery or project our frustrations on our 'sisters'. Whether you are holding hurt or hurling hurt, there is hope! So what negative thoughts are you projecting or holding on to? Can you see the way out that Jesus is offering? How might you be able to stop and sit with him?

5

Contagion

Although battles between women can seem personal and private, when viewed with the gift of hindsight they can often show significant influence on others – a contagion beyond expectations, a disease that can spread like wildfire. We can escape comparison's grip the way a healthy immune system protects us from a deadly virus.

The apostle Paul was no stranger to disagreements. Originally named Saul, he was at the forefront of the Jewish opposition to the growing Christian religion. On a journey to persecute a new group of Christ-followers, he was stopped in his tracks by a vision of Jesus Christ. The abrupt light-bulb moment caused Paul to see that he was working not on behalf of God but in opposition. He submitted to the purposes of Jesus and began preaching the gospel, planting churches and encouraging Christ-followers both in person and via letters. The letters, rich in wisdom, teaching and the Holy Spirit, remain as relevant today as they were then.

One of Paul's letters was written to the believers in Philippi while he was under house arrest in Rome. In Philippians, as with many of his letters, Paul uses the 'signing-off' sentences as a chance to honour, commend, encourage and challenge – sometimes actually naming individuals.

Drawing his letter to a conclusion, Paul writes:

Therefore, my dear brothers and sisters, stay true to the Lord. I love you and long to see you, dear friends, for you are my joy and the crown I receive for my work.

> Now I appeal to Euodia and Syntyche. Please, because you belong to the Lord, settle your disagreement. And I ask you, my true partner, to help these two women, for they worked hard with me in telling others the Good News. They worked along with Clement and the rest of my co-workers, whose names are written in the Book of Life.
>
> Always be full of joy in the Lord. I say it again – rejoice! (Philippians 4.1–4)

It is easy to miss, but tucked in between the encouragement to stay aligned with the Lord and to know the joy of the Lord, two women are urged to settle a disagreement. We don't know who the 'true partner' is, but for Euodia and Syntyche there is no hiding! This is the only time that these women are named but, goodness, what a way to go down in history – because of a disagreement! Not much is known about these women but scholars have been able to deduce some things.

Paul was a leader who recognized gift before gender and encouraged female leadership. These women had been mission leaders alongside Paul and his co-workers to spread the gospel of Christ, yet now that ministry was under threat because of their disagreement.

Paul does not write as someone who has never experienced relational breakdown. He is not personally immune from relational disagreements. In fact he had a disagreement with Barnabas, over the involvement of a young disciple called Mark, that was described in Acts as 'so sharp'.[1] Barnabas and Paul went their separate ways for a season. However, the disagreement doesn't seem to impinge upon their mission to share the good news of Jesus. His experience gives him a greater authority to challenge the women, and his wholehearted followership of Jesus gives him confidence they too can find the way through this.

Paul knew Jesus taught that to come to him with an open heart people must be in good standing with those around them. What we carry in our hearts from bitterness, resentment, hurts and anger will have an impact on our relationship with Christ, impeding our intimacy with him.

> You have heard that our ancestors were told, 'You must not murder. If you commit murder, you are subject to judgment.' But I say, if you are even angry with someone, you are subject to judgment! If you call someone an idiot, you are in danger of being brought before the court. And if you curse someone, you are in danger of the fires of hell.
>
> So if you are presenting a sacrifice at the altar in the Temple and you suddenly remember that someone has something against you, leave your sacrifice there at the altar. Go and be reconciled to that person. Then come and offer your sacrifice to God. (Matthew 5.21–24)

Euodia and Syntyche's disagreement was clearly having a negative impact on the church, toxically moving through the body like a virus spreading division. Paul doesn't take sides but simply urges them, with the support of a mediator, to choose to settle their disagreement. The original language shows Paul urging them to be 'of the same mind'. In other words, this is an intentional choice going beyond and being independent of feelings.

Paul says that both Euodia and Syntyche worked 'along with Clement and the rest of my co-workers, whose names are written in the Book of Life' (Philippians 4.3): co-workers, on the mission all Christ-followers share, to go and make disciples. From the privileged position of salvation, they were commissioned to reach out and help others find Christ too. Paul, referring to their names as being in the 'Book of Life', shows that Euodia and Syntyche are saved. However, perhaps this has a challenge with it too. Was their bickering and feuding limiting their relationship with Christ, and was it limiting other people from finding Christ – having *their* names added to the

Book of Life? Heaven forbid that our earthly disagreements prevent other people from discovering a living, saving relationship with Christ.

Just imagine these ladies chatting about their disagreement with people in and outside of the church community. Isn't it possible that people might end up choosing sides and getting drawn into the ruptured relationship? The church could end up looking ridiculous through the picture they were painting of it, and some people might be put off connecting. This is a challenge – remember the analogy that Jesus is the groom and the Church is his bride? To know the groom well we cannot ignore his bride. So were Euodia and Syntyche risking ruining people's desire to get to know the bride – and helping them to miss meeting the groom?

In another letter, Paul wrote to Timothy, saying,

> Again I say, don't get involved in foolish, ignorant arguments that only start fights. A servant of the Lord must not quarrel but must be kind to everyone, be able to teach, and be patient with difficult people. Gently instruct those who oppose the truth. Perhaps God will change those people's hearts, and they will learn the truth. Then they will come to their senses and escape from the devil's trap. For they have been held captive by him to do whatever he wants.
> (2 Timothy 2.23–26)

Are women being drawn into sharing disagreements in such a way that other people are being prevented from experiencing the love of Christ? Are we trying to win arguments that the Lord never wanted us to engage with in the first place?

Is the opinion you are holding against another so valuable that it is worth risking blocking someone else from finding Jesus or blocking yourself from being all that the Lord has intended and created you for? In this Philippians passage, when Paul is citing the women, he emphasizes that they helped him spread the good news – speaking to their purpose or spiritual identity – but all that was probably on hold because of the feud. It was becoming a part of history, not their future! Feuding will prohibit the purpose of the Lord being realized both for and beyond the feuding parties. We must not let divisions divert people from their divine destinies.

Jesus taught his followers to recognize the enemy's role in their lives, describing Satan as a thief, saying: 'The thief's purpose is to steal and kill and destroy. My purpose is to give them a rich and satisfying life' (John 10.10).

Were Euodia and Syntyche experiencing life to the full in its richness and satisfaction? Undoubtedly – no! Were they having their joy and peace stolen and destroyed? Undoubtedly – yes! So, was the enemy involved in making matters worse for them and the wider Church? Yes!

When Paul wrote to the believers in Ephesus he reminded them to

Be strong in the Lord and in his mighty power. Put on all of God's armour so that you will be able to stand firm against all strategies of the devil. For we are not fighting against flesh-and-blood enemies, but against evil rulers and authorities of the unseen world, against mighty powers in this dark world, and against evil spirits in the heavenly places.

Therefore, put on every piece of God's armour so you will be able to resist the enemy in the time of evil. Then after the battle you will still be standing firm. Stand your ground, putting on the belt of truth and the body armour of God's righteousness. For shoes, put on the peace that comes from the Good News so that you will be fully prepared. In addition to all of these, hold up the shield of faith to stop the fiery arrows of the devil. Put on salvation as your helmet, and take the sword of the Spirit, which is the word of God.

Pray in the Spirit at all times and on every occasion. Stay alert and be persistent in your prayers for all believers everywhere.
(Ephesians 6.10–18)

If Euodia and Syntyche had recognized that their enemies were first and foremost not each other, not even human but spiritual, just imagine what fallout might have been averted. If they had recognized the enemy's activities disguised in human form and responded by relying on the Lord . . . If, if, if . . .

Comparison, jealousy, disappointment and regrets will become like clothes to us, and when we put them on they will prevent us from putting on the armour of God. It is like trying to take hold of something when your hands are already full. First we have to let go, take off, all that restricts, in order to put on the freedoms and spiritual defences available to us. This might seem impossible to you right now but as we proceed you will come to see the freedom that you can engage in. More on this later.

When it came to disagreements and the challenges in relating to others, Jesus was noticeably specific.

First, in the area of forgiveness, when asked how many times we must forgive the same person he took the basic maths and pretty much answered with the equivalent of infinity. For eternity our forgiveness factor is to the power of infinity! 'Peter came to him and asked, "Lord, how often should I forgive someone who sins against me? Seven times?" "No, not seven times," Jesus replied, "but seventy times seven!"' (Matthew 18.21–22).

Forgiveness does not say that something wrong is suddenly right, but rather that forgiveness is needed because of the recognition that something wrong has occurred. You don't need to forgive someone for good things! Nor does it suddenly induce some form of spiritual amnesia so that something is no longer able to be recalled. Forgive and forget are not partners, but forgive and choose not to recall are.

Nor does forgiveness indicate that there won't still be consequences to work out. However, forgiveness will stop the contagion from spreading and will stop the enemy from being given permission to steal, kill and destroy more.

Jesus taught his disciples about handling disagreements, because he knew they would happen.

> If another believer sins against you, go privately and point out the offence. If the other person listens and confesses it, you have won that person back. But if you are unsuccessful, take one or two others with you and go back again, so that everything you say may be confirmed by two or three witnesses. If the person still refuses to listen, take your case to the church. Then if he or she won't accept the church's decision, treat that person as a pagan or a corrupt tax collector.
>
> I tell you the truth, whatever you forbid on earth will be forbidden in heaven, and whatever you permit on earth will be permitted in heaven.
>
> I also tell you this: If two of you agree here on earth concerning anything you ask, my Father in heaven will do it for you. For where two or three gather together as my followers, I am there among them.
> (Matthew 18.15–20)

Have you ever wondered what it might take for your prayers to be answered? Have you considered that sometimes our prayers lose power simply because we are at odds, not with God, but with another woman? Just imagine what might happen if we allowed ourselves to dare to disarm, to align with God's plan for his daughters and choose unity. Perhaps because of the significance of how women can compete and compare, it becomes particularly difficult when forgiveness is needed with regard to another woman. Are we more reluctant to extend forgiveness to a woman than we might be to a man? If there is any particular tendency in us to withhold for-giveness from women, or a particular woman, then we would be wise to address this in order not to prohibit our own freedom and purposes in Christ.

We will come back to forgiveness and how we need the help of other women later on. In the meantime, let's have a quick personal health check. Have you succumbed to the contagion effect of some other women's disagreements? Are you preventing someone from meeting the groom because you are so busy holding on to offences with the bride? Paul knew that Euodia and Syntyche needed a third person to help them through to freedom – so maybe you need to get someone to help you to 'come to one mind' with *her* as well!

6

Conspiracy

When I opened the email from a friend I was unaware that I was just about to open some personal 'mind chatter' and an over-thinking destructive spiral. My friend thought it prudent to tell me that she had seen some women enjoying a head-to-head over a coffee. This alone is not newsworthy but for the fact that we were working through a challenging situation which involved one of these women, and there was a strong suspicion that the others were being 'recruited' into her disgruntled and divisive dialogue. I had no facts to substantiate any real concerns, just the well-intended email from a friend and a personal knowledge of the wider backstory.

However, my clicking 'open' triggered a spiral. For the next few days my brain went into overdrive. I scripted their conversation. I stalked them on social media to scrutinize behaviour. This proved emotionally catalytic because I then realized I'd been 'unfriended' and launched my own pity party and full-on conspiracy theory that these women were launching an unfriending-missile attack against me. I must have switched between social media platforms, checking their movements, about 50 times in as many hours! Were they talking about me? What were they thinking about me? Did they hate me? Why did they hate me? Why were they being so harsh and assuming the worst of me? Who else were they talking to about me? Why were they lying about me? If they had a problem with me why didn't they just come and talk with me?

From an email about *them* it became all about *me*! Spying via social media is rarely helpful and what I was doing was certainly not healthy. It was definitely not life-giving to me. And bless them – these women knew nothing about it and were most probably simply enjoying a latte and a bit of life together. There were 500 million things they could have been talking about and yet, somewhat arrogantly and self-centredly, I assumed that *I* was the most important topic of conversation!

US preacher Rick Warren is attributed as saying, 'Humility is not thinking less of yourself, it's thinking of yourself less.' In this situation I definitely would have benefited from thinking about myself less.

I was proving the science that my mind has a huge capacity to focus on negative thoughts. Was I single-handedly fuelling a conspiracy that I was being wronged?

When Paul wrote to the Galatians he highlighted the human propensity to produce a whole load of rubbish without much effort! The fruit produced from a human life without divine intervention is a disappointing list. Look at how this is described in *The Message*'s paraphrase:

> It is obvious what kind of life develops out of trying to get your own way all the time: repetitive, loveless, cheap sex; a stinking accumulation of mental and emotional garbage; frenzied and joyless grabs for happiness; trinket gods; magic-show religion; paranoid loneliness; cutthroat competition; all-consuming-yet-never-satisfied wants; a brutal temper; an impotence to love or be loved; divided homes and divided lives; small-minded and lopsided pursuits; the vicious habit of depersonalizing everyone into a rival; uncontrolled and uncontrollable addictions; ugly parodies of community. I could go on.
> (Galatians 5.19–21, *The Message*)

Oh my gosh, girls – this is not good reading, is it? I was definitely suffering from a 'stinking accumulation of mental and emotional garbage' from the news that these ladies were having a coffee!

But before we become focused on the rubbish we can generate in our lives, let's remember what we looked at when discussing Euodia and Syntyche. Whether we have previously been aware of this or not, we have a real enemy and he enjoys creating monuments out of the moments! Even in the middle of disasters our enemy will try and make it a defining destiny that will restrict our future.

To understand this fully, let's remind ourselves of the creation narrative. God had created everything and it was all good. Yet right into the middle of the Garden of Eden – disguised in that snakeskin – came the enemy. There he tricked Eve into satisfying her hunger for the knowledge of good and evil (and Adam joined in). The immediate ramifications were a sudden, terrifying awareness of their shame to such an extent that they tried to hide from God.

It is worth noting that the resulting consequences for Eve were huge and would have their impact on all future generations, as God said to the serpent, 'I will cause hostility between you and the woman, and between your offspring and her offspring' (Genesis 3.15). Offspring will of course not be limited to only women, but right here is a dramatic revelation of the enemy's particular animosity towards women!

In my privileged Western context, could the enemy be trapping me into battles of comparison and jealousy? Could those around me or you be trapped in his animosity? How about on a global scale?

In *Half the Sky*, authors Nicholas Kristof and Sheryl WuDunn have observed the violence that is targeted at women:

The global statistics on the abuse of girls are numbing. It appears that more girls have been killed in the last fifty years, precisely because they were girls, than men were killed in all the battles of the twentieth century. More girls are killed in this routine 'gendercide' in any one decade than people were slaughtered in all the genocides of the twentieth century.[1]

Kristof and WuDunn continue that 'women aren't the problem but the solution. The plight of girls is no more a tragedy than an opportunity.'[2]

The Western problems I face are arguably trivial in comparison to the atrocities some of our sisters experience in other places. But if we hold on to our battles with our close neighbours and sisters we will never be part of the solution and help a stranger!

Kristof and WuDunn recognized that

honour killings, sexual slavery, and genital cutting may seem to Western readers to be tragic but inevitable in a world far, far away. In much the same way, slavery was once widely viewed by many decent Europeans and Americans as a regrettable but ineluctable feature of human life. It was just one more horror that had existed for thousands of years. But then in the 1780s a few indignant Britons, led by William Wilberforce, decided that slavery was so offensive that they had to abolish it. And they did. Today we see the seed of something similar: a global movement to emancipate women and girls.[3]

The spectrum of assaults against women is as vast and different as the number of women in the world. I'm sure many of us would like to be part of the solution that liberates those women suffering the most extreme of abuses, and by God's grace we will. But unless we wake up to the enemy's conspiracy and recognize the battles that are closer to home, this work will always be limited.

When we sleepwalk our way through life and don't wake up to the enemy's schemes, then we will remain in the grip of jealousy and comparison and limit our effectiveness to be able to truly help others to their freedom.

When I opened *that* email and allowed my thoughts to spiral into an inner conflict, I inadvertently aligned with the enemy's conspiracy against women – me and those latte-friends. I allowed myself to be hurt and negatively emotionally attacked their reputations – albeit in my head! I know no one died. No one was physically hurt. But this is the challenge – we will not win the war that is against women if we don't win this battle. Until we can discover the freedom that is ours when we escape the grip of jealousy and grow in our concern for our nearby sisters to experience freedom, how will we muster the concern required to help other women discover their freedom from their prisons too? How will we help the girls-around-the-globe if we harbour such jealousy against the girls-next-door?

So are you up for this revolution? Ready to tackle the battles close to home? Can we recognize the traps we are caught in now and discover the freedom that is available? Can we embrace this challenge that it's time to help each other escape the comparison trap?

The good news is that Jesus came for us all, his grace is sufficient, he alone provides the way out required and he alone reverses the curse!

Next we're going to look at some of the most contested relationships in the workplace. Whether your 'workplace' is a place of employment, school, college, home or elsewhere, there will be something here for you too.

Part 2
BOSSING IT

7
Work at *whatever*

A few decades ago an employee might have expected to hold a job for life. Professions such as banking or education often meant that from leaving school through to retiring, career progression happened in one sphere – maybe even one location. Today things are very different. The average person is likely to change jobs 10 to 15 times in a lifetime. This is not simply working your way *up* a ladder: this is more like traversing the scaffolding and maybe moving up while you are on your way. Navigating through a lifetime of work rather than being focused constantly on an upward trajectory enables a career to be rich in variety and diverse in experiences, and provides a framework for a wide set of skills to be developed.

I've done my fair share of traversing – secretarial temp, youth and student worker, various roles in hotels, sales assistant in a wholefood wholesaler, childminding, teaching assistant, church leader, speaker, author.

Apparently in the approximately 50-year period of employment the average person working full time will spend the equivalent of 13 years and two months at work.[1] If you found yourself working for Jack Ma, the Chinese billionaire and co-founder of the online shopping giant Alibaba, you would work for decidedly more time, because he apparently continues to argue for a 9.00 a.m. to 9.00 p.m. working day, over a six-day week.[2] That's a lot of hours to clock up and demonstrates a life philosophy of 'living to work rather than working to live'.

Of course, for some of us work changes over the years can include gaps for sick leave, adoption or maternity leave, carer's leave or other such breaks.

With so many hours dedicated to work it is no wonder that work-based relationships are significant, and when it comes to females our working relationships with each other can fall anywhere on the spectrum between brilliant and embattled!

Over these next few chapters we're going to explore working relationships between women. We're going to take an honest look at how things sometimes are and how God might be able to make things better. There will be plenty that is relevant to you – even if you are not in paid employment.

The Bible has something to say about pretty much everything, and work is definitely one of the topics. You won't find specifics on where to work but there is plenty of wisdom to glean about *how* we work. And if you feel as though you've been working like a slave recently then the biblical language might be even easier to relate to!

Paul wrote about work to the believers in Ephesus[3] and sent a similar message to the believers in Colossae, saying,

> Slaves, obey your earthly masters in everything you do. Try to please them all the time, not just when they are watching you. Serve them sincerely because of your reverent fear of the Lord. Work willingly at whatever you do, as though you were working for the Lord rather than for people. Remember that the Lord will give you an inheritance as your reward, and that the Master you are serving is Christ. But if you do what is wrong, you will be paid back for the wrong you have done. For God has no favourites. Masters, be just and fair to your slaves. Remember that you also have a Master – in heaven.
> (Colossians 3.22—4.1)

Understanding the Bible requires understanding the first-century context in which the original text was written before we apply it to our own situations. So having a message sent to two communities where followers of Christ might be either slave or slave-master is significant. For us in the twenty-first century we can consider that, whether we are employee or employer, God is as interested in *how* we work as *what* work we do. In fact, when our 'how' lines up with God's best we will find 'what' we do comes in line with his best plans too.

With regard to our working relationships, there are at least two significant pieces of wisdom we can glean from Paul's letters. First, the encouragement from Paul to the Christ-followers was to work at *whatever you do* in such a way that brings glory to God. So whether you are the boss or the employee, how you work can bring God glory. Whether you have reached the top of the ladder or feel as though you are scrambling around trying to reach up to the bottom rung, are working in the dream job or the one of nightmares, *how* you work is significant. Whether you feel as if you are remunerated generously, part of the all-star team on a public platform, or working more in isolation and scraping to make ends meet, with no one paying attention to your efforts – *how* you are working matters. The encouragement is to work at *whatever* you do in such a way that you become a living signpost for the Lord. We should work for the Lord's glory even if no one else seems to notice. Discovering *how* we work in our places of employment is as critical, if not more so, as discovering *what* we are going to do as a choice of career. Refining your transferable employment *attitudes* as much as focusing on your skills means that you can be consistent in *how* you work at *whatever* you do.

This is made possible by the second principle Paul introduced. Having looked at how people worked, he then introduced the idea of *who* they really worked for. For the slaves, he encouraged them to remember that it was the Lord who would ultimately reward their work. Even though for every day of hard labour they were not on the receiving end of reasonable remuneration, the Lord would ultimately reward them. For the masters, he urged them to remember that they too worked for Christ.

How we choose to work and remembering who we really work for will have a significant impact on our relationships with each other in the workplace. Whether we have a boss or are the boss, we are all ultimately able to work for the Lord. This is all beautifully demonstrated by a story written long ago in the second book of Kings.

In 2 Kings 5 is the story of Naaman, the army commander of the armies of Ben-Hadad II, the king of Aram-Damascus and the enemy of Israel. Naaman was a powerful and successful warrior, but he was suffering from leprosy. The story tells how

> Aramean raiders had invaded the land of Israel, and among their captives was a young girl who had been given to Naaman's wife as a maid. One day the girl said to her mistress, 'I wish my master would go to see the prophet in Samaria. He would heal him of his leprosy.'
> (2 Kings 5.2–3)

Mark Greene of the London Institute of Contemporary Christianity summarizes the slave girl's situation:

> the girl with no name is captured and ends up as a slave in a pagan household, in a pagan land, working for the enemy commander's pagan wife . . . she is in the wrong job, the wrong place, with the wrong people, with the wrong present and the wrong future. Where, oh where, she must have wondered, is God in all of this? How she must have yearned to be somewhere else.[4]

Instead of being bitter and grouchy at her loss of freedom, this young girl gave her best into her workplace and spoke a confident message of hope to her mistress. God can heal leprosy! This girl with no name knew that the person who stole her could find his own freedom from suffering if he would but reach out to God. Gently, yet confidently, she spoke a message of hope into a hopeless situation.

Our workplace will, most probably, be worlds apart from the context this young girl in Aram endured. However, if she, and the slaves in Colossae, could find a way to reflect the Lord's heart for the people around them, then we can too! How we remain teachable by the Lord and aware of him is at the heart of real success in the workplace. The quality of our attitude and our work will reflect the condition of our hearts. If we've taken resources from our workplace without permission, claimed a sick day when we've not been sick, stolen credit for someone else's great idea or work, spread a rumour or spoken badly of people behind their backs, then we are not demonstrating God's fullest love for our colleagues. God does not want his grace kept a secret from our colleagues.

As Mark Greene encourages his readers to make the most of their workplace mission opportunities, he says,

> there are all kinds of ways we demonstrate the difference Jesus makes in our lives and all kinds of ways we can serve people through our actions, but the people on our frontline also need to hear that it was Jesus who made the difference to us and that Jesus is the only one who can make an eternal difference to them.[5]

How we work and speak in our workplace is hugely significant as we strive to see the fulfilment of the kingdom opportunities that our position provides. Into this opportunity can come one of the greatest challenges for some of us – how we relate to the other women that we work with!

There has been a huge amount of study invested in how women work together. There seem to be two distinct contexts that really do make a huge difference to how we relate and what battles we will experience. These contexts are whether it is a predominantly female working environment, with women at all levels of responsibility and authority, or whether it is a largely male-dominated environment, with men holding the majority of senior responsibilities.

There is evidence that women who work in a male-dominated environment are less likely to express solidarity with other female employees. This can lead to intensifying competition between women.[6] However, where working environments are more equal between men and women, the women apparently have more solidarity.

This is because women in a male-dominated environment feel that they are vying for promotion against other women, rather than their male peers, and therefore women are a threat to their opportunities. This leads to tokenism. When there are few opportunities for women, other than a token position, then women can view their gender as an impediment.

Tokenism facilitates the idea that only exceptional women will make it through the ranks and to the top – whatever the top actually is!

This feeling of tokenism can lead to what is called 'favouritism threat'.[7] Women can experience concern that they will be seen as biased if they help one another. As a result, women can apparently think that the way to get ahead is to distance themselves from other women and instead blend in with men. But blending in with men creates a whole new set of biases and problems, including blending in with others rather than standing out as a unique person, adopting behavioural patterns from an unwritten code of conduct and favouring male colleagues at the expense of the women.

There is a psychological concept called system justification.[8] This happens when oppressed groups of people struggle to make sense of an unfair world and as a result internalize negative stereotypes. Once internalized, that stereotype becomes the normalized way of thinking. So if an employment situation is unfair towards a

particular people group they can begin to develop negative stereotypes which become increasingly reinforced in their minds. If a working environment is male dominated, with fewer opportunities being open to women, pay inequalities based on gender, and promotions and personal development being less accessible for women, then it is possible for women to feel oppressed and to internalize negative stereotypes in their thinking. It is a context that sets up women to experience acrimony in their relationships, seeing each other as a threat.

Whether positive change happens in the near or distant future, are there ways in which we, as women, can consider how we are working with one another and look for opportunities for improvement? Friends, relating and working with other women in the contexts we find ourselves – how are we doing?

There is a stereotype that female bosses can be hard to work for. Male bosses can be affirmed as being strong, whereas a strong female boss gets criticized for being bossy or striving. Male bosses seem to be given extra latitude, and there is an expectation that they will be frank, but female bosses are expected somehow to soften their language.

This all poses a significant challenge to those of us women who are leaders. How can we both use and grow our gift of leadership, fulfilling our God-given mandate? Change is always required, but how can we do that by way of honouring God rather than merely appeasing stereotypical expectations?

Can we reject society's expectations and truly meet and lead people, beginning from where they are?

For those not in leadership roles, the challenge is how to encourage rather than undermine a female leader, to see her form of leadership not as stereotypical hardness but as confidence and strength.

Some female employees are reported to prefer a male boss because they have a perception that female bosses are more bullying.

53

Sometimes a bossy female boss will be described as a 'Queen Bee Boss' – her sting is scary and potentially deadly. Some women believe that women bosses are always vicious, but this is an unfair caricature reinforcing an employment narrative against women in senior positions of authority and responsibility. If your workplace has the primal philosophy that men hold the power of impregnation, whether it be for babies, bonuses or promotion, then women will prefer a male boss because of the rewards.

Evolutionary psychologists have studied the nature–nurture theory for many years. Are people the product of their surroundings or of some internal 'wirings', a DNA pattern that is uncontrollable? There is general recognition that there is a human instinct for survival, whether it be channelled towards productive sexual partnering or employment promotions.

This, of course, is nothing new to the Christian. In the early Genesis narratives, the writer captures the essence of God's frustration with the human condition that has a propensity towards self and away from him:

> The LORD observed the extent of human wickedness on the earth, and he saw that everything they thought or imagined was consistently and totally evil. So the LORD was sorry he had ever made them and put them on the earth. It broke his heart.
>
> (Genesis 6.5–6)

This theme is later picked up by Paul when he recognizes that 'The trouble is with me, for I am all too human, a slave to sin. I don't really understand myself, for I want to do what is right, but I don't do it. Instead, I do what I hate' (Romans 7.14–15).

Can we acknowledge that within each of us is the capacity to veer towards selfish primal survival urges, and to have the inner subconscious desire to succeed and be personally recognized for our contribution? We all have the tendency to consider that our reward is best received when issued from human superiors. Do you find yourself striving and competing in your place of work or study?

We have the capacity to compete with those we perceive as our opposition and threat, so how can we make sure we don't hurt people along the way and, even more importantly, how can we work at whatever we do in such a way that it brings God glory?

8

You are seen

In considering our working relationships with other women we can draw wisdom from a biblical story of brokenness, barrenness and battlegrounds between two very different women. There are particular insights we can obtain by looking at the relationship between a servant and a mistress which compare usefully with what we might experience as an employee or a boss.

In the background of the Bible stories of the forefather of faith, Abram, is a tenacious and tough lady who endured years of journeying under the shadow of cultural disgrace. Sarai's barrenness would have been interpreted by many as a sign of the Lord responding to her sins by closing her womb and turning away from her. Perhaps she felt the silent treatment from her Lord and sensed the suspicious judgement of her companions. Abram was always seen as favoured, faithful and courageous in his pursuit of the Lord's calling. Yet barrenness accompanied them every step along the way.

In *The Resolution for Women*, author and motivational speaker Priscilla Shirer describes the depth of longing a woman can experience in childlessness as 'perhaps something even deeper in a woman's psyche than the desire to find her heart's true love'.[1]

For the 99-year-old Sarai, although the physical capacity to carry a child had long passed, the deep longing still hadn't. So she came up with a 'plan B'. She thought outside their physical limitations and with that came the introduction of a new woman in Sarai's story – Hagar. Sarai was going to come to regret this decision, but nonetheless at the time it seemed like a workable solution.

Sarai said to Abram, 'The LORD has prevented me from having children. Go and sleep with my servant. Perhaps I can have children through her.' And Abram agreed with Sarai's proposal. So Sarai, Abram's wife, took Hagar the Egyptian servant and gave her to Abram as a wife.
(Genesis 16.2–3)

The Lord had made it clear that a direct birth-descendant would be his heir, not a child of a servant. At this point Abram had not discussed the specifics with the Lord.

Sarai and Hagar's relationship was just about to enter into a highly contested, mutually painful season. However, before we look at that we're going to pause and look at how Hagar might have joined Sarai's household as her servant.

We know that Abram, under the Lord's direct instructions, left his father's family and headed in the direction of Canaan, as the Lord showed them. Unfortunately, Canaan suffered a severe famine which necessitated Abram and Sarai pressing on to Egypt in a quest for survival.

Aware that they were foreigners in a strange land, Abram was concerned for their safety. He came up with a plan to pretend to be brother and sister rather than husband and wife and so less of a threat to the 'top man'.

Whether it was the tone and texture of her hair, the colour of her skin, the shape of her eyes or the curve of her nose, Sarai's beauty was not the same as Egyptian beauty and heads turned towards her, noticing the differences. As with many patriarchal traditions, the top man could take anyone he chose, and clearly many people enjoyed the opportunity of telling Egypt's top man there was a new girl in town!

Sure enough, when Abram arrived in Egypt, everyone noticed Sarai's beauty. When the palace officials saw her, they sang her praises to Pharaoh, their king, and Sarai was taken into his palace. Then Pharaoh gave Abram many gifts because of her – sheep, goats, cattle, male and female donkeys, male and female servants, and camels.

(Genesis 12.14–16)

So not only did Abram survive, they were able to thrive as they gained wealth!

However, God didn't seem as thrilled with the arrangement and sent 'terrible plagues upon Pharaoh and his household because of Sarai' (Genesis 12.17), and so angrily and fearfully Pharaoh made sure that Abram and Sarai were escorted out of his country!

The Bible does not say when Hagar joined Sarai and Abram. Jewish interpreters and commentators on the Old Testament, writing in what is referred to as the Midrash,[2] introduce us to this fascinating woman. Here, according to the Midrash, Pharaoh extended unmerited favour by not killing Abram or Sarai. This did not go unnoticed by others in the palace, and Pharaoh's own daughter observed that 'It is better to be a slave in Sarah's house than a princess in my own.'[3]

While the practice of slavery is not something that sits well in our cultural context today, there is a biblical theme that recognizes the benefits of being a slave to the right person, which surpasses freedoms with the wrong people. As the lost son realized when he came to his senses in the pig-pen of prodigal living,

At home even the hired servants have food enough to spare, and here I am dying of hunger! I will go home to my father and say, 'Father, I have sinned against both heaven and you, and I am no longer worthy of being called your son. Please take me on as a hired servant.'

(Luke 15.17–19)

Also Psalm 84:

> Better is one day in your courts
>   than a thousand elsewhere;
> I would rather be a doorkeeper in the house of my God
>   than dwell in the tents of the wicked.
> (Psalm 84.10, NIV)

Living in the company of the wicked as described in the temporary accommodation of 'tents' (even if those tents are actually palaces!) cannot exceed the benefits offered to a slave when in the house of the Lord.

So it is not inconceivable that, even if as a woman she did not have the power to really choose, Hagar was willing to leave the palace and serve Sarai because of the favour that she saw was on Sarai's life.

Perhaps Hagar had wanted what Sarai could give her: she wanted to come under her anointing. However, she had yet to learn the true hardships that Sarai had endured and the journey she was on. She had yet to realize that great wine is only produced when good grapes are crushed! This is a potential tension we experience, too, between admiring another woman and being jealous of her at the same time.

The young Egyptian Hagar then came under the cover, the protection, the favour and the employ of Sarai, and this perhaps exceeded the experience she was having as a member of the king's household in the Egyptian palace. Ancient commentators say that, under the escort of her father's soldiers, she left Egypt in the company of Abram and Sarai. According to the Midrash, Hagar's name originated here, coming from *Ha-Gar*, meaning 'this is the reward'. But as we all know, while gifts are unmerited, rewards are earned!

Hagar stayed close to Sarai while under her employ. She was young and apparently helpful, and was able to stay in the eyeline of Sarai, not drifting to the periphery but staying close. So when

Sarai was thinking of new solutions to their heirless predicament, Hagar was in view.

The writer of Genesis captures the pivotal moment where the tension between these women really started: 'So Abram had sexual relations with Hagar, and she became pregnant. But when Hagar knew she was pregnant, she began to treat her mistress, Sarai, with contempt' (Genesis 16.4).

Hagar's heart hardened. Coldness crept over her towards her mistress and she felt elevated to a higher ground. She was no longer subject to her mistress, not even just an equal – she considered herself better than Sarai. The 'golden ticket' to her future was now within her. In reality, her pregnancy promoted her to a senior position, as the provision of an heir could make her son even 'higher' than Sarai.

Hagar had no respect for the 'family court' view of her position and she looked down on the woman she had once looked up to. Sarai was no longer on Hagar's pedestal of favour but had been torn down and held in contempt. The woman she once held in high regard was now held in disregard.

Hagar's contempt for her mistress hurt Sarai. It was like rubbing salt into an open wound. The person Sarai had brought into her inner circle and in whom she had put her hope was choosing to crush her, demean her and boast of her own swelling bump.

Having agreed to Sarai's original request, Abram appeared to not want to get involved again, nor come between the two women. When Sarai complained to him about Hagar he backed out and simply encouraged Sarai to do whatever she wanted. 'Look, she is your servant, so deal with her as you see fit' (Genesis 16.6).

I'm not sure Sarai knew how to 'see fit' at this stage. Can anyone 'see fit' when they are so hurt by disappointment and the subject of such contempt? Sarai's barrenness was compounded by a sense of betrayal as all the years of pain were exacerbated by the boastful contempt of her maidservant. Perhaps the well-worn phrase of 'hurt people hurt people' rang true, for Sarai is said to have treated Hagar 'so harshly that she finally ran away' (Genesis 16.6).

Oh, the anguish of these two women as their relationship spiralled into a war that could have been avoided.

It is often said that in trauma people will choose fight, flight or freeze. For young Hagar, the fight seemed pointless and flight seemed a viable option. However, this story is not over. The Lord was not finished with Hagar and in fact had a lot to say to her as she tried to flee. The Lord questioned her as if he didn't know the answer – perhaps he wanted to know that she knew the answer, to hear her say it. Her experience had hurt her, yet the Lord wanted to draw her closer to him in the middle of her wilderness.

This young woman from Egypt pauses in the wilderness by a fresh spring and has an encounter with the Lord – an encounter that will send her back to her mistress, seen, heard, valued, loved and empowered, an encounter that will assure her of her future, and that of her son – even though his future is still unknown!

> The angel of the LORD found Hagar beside a spring of water in the wilderness, along the road to Shur. The angel said to her, 'Hagar, Sarai's servant, where have you come from, and where are you going?'
>
> 'I'm running away from my mistress, Sarai,' she replied.
>
> The angel of the LORD said to her, 'Return to your mistress, and submit to her authority.' Then he added, 'I will give you more descendants than you can count.'
>
> (Genesis 16.7–10)

'Where have you come from?' might seem a simple question to Hagar, running away from her mistress. However, I think there is more to it. I think the Lord is inviting Hagar to have longer recall, to remember more than simply the recent mistreatment from Sarai. Perhaps he wants her to look in her own heart and take responsibility for the contempt growing within her alongside the growing unborn child in her womb. The condition of Hagar's heart is no one's responsibility other than her own. While Sarai is responsible for her own actions and attitudes, Hagar is responsible for her own response to them. Perhaps the Lord wants to remind her of the kindness, protection, favour that Sarai has previously extended to her over many years and to help her extend grace and compassion to her mistress in replacement for the contempt. Submission brings humility rather than the pride of contempt.

We might identify with Hagar and feel her pain at being so harshly treated in our places of employment. We might be keen to justify her choice of behaviour and even the running away. Yet from Hagar's story we can see God is more interested in the condition of our hearts, from which our behaviour flows. God is not simply wanting a relationship for behaviour management. He wants our hearts healed, tender and trusting. He longs for our wholeness so that we can actively engage with him and the relationships around us rather than flee and hide. Hagar wanted to run away from the pain but the Lord encouraged her to run *to him* and then face the pain *with him*.

Even as Hagar was encouraged to go back and talk, clear the air, reach out and be restored, so perhaps the same challenge is ours. There might not be relational carnage in your rear-view mirror but who might the Lord encourage you to reconnect with? What selective memories might the Lord want to speak to? Hagar was so keen to blame Sarai, but the Lord was not interested in entering into that conversation – wholeness, healing and restoration (in spite of Sarai's actions) were on the Lord's heart for Hagar.

Many years later Jesus would teach his disciples, telling them,

And why worry about a speck in your friend's eye when you have a log in your own? How can you think of saying to your friend, 'Let me help you get rid of that speck in your eye,' when

you can't see past the log in your own eye? Hypocrite! First get rid of the log in your own eye; then you will see well enough to deal with the speck in your friend's eye.'
(Matthew 7.3–5)

The truth of the parable is that, with grace, both the friend's 'speck' and person's own 'log' can be removed, but our own eye-logs are our own responsibility! *She* might have wronged you but what are you responsible for in the relationship? What can you bring to the Lord in authentic openness to his love?

Hagar in the wilderness faced some difficult truths as she searched her soul. Conceived within her spirit was contempt for her mistress, because Hagar had claimed a position of authority that was not hers to claim. The Lord wasn't dealing harshly with her, forcing his judgement, but rather wanting to express his love for her, letting her know that there was more for her, that there was better for her. She might well have been on the receiving end of mistreatment; however, that particular 'speck' was surpassed by the 'log' of her contempt. The Lord sent her back to try again.

But she was not to rush back without fully embracing the encounter with the Lord. Hagar was told to name her son 'Ishmael (which means "God hears"), for the LORD has heard your cry of distress' (Genesis 16.11). She paused in this place and felt a heavenly hug from the Father.

From that moment on, Hagar referred to the Lord as El-roi:

Thereafter, Hagar used another name to refer to the LORD, who had spoken to her. She said, 'You are the God who sees me.' She also said, 'Have I truly seen the One who sees me?' So that well was named Beer-lahai-roi (which means 'well of the Living One who sees me'). It can still be found between Kadesh and Bered.
(Genesis 16.13–14)

This is beautiful! The Egyptian girl encountered the Living God and knew that she was accepted, loved, forgiven, heard and seen! There is no wilderness place or time of day that the Lord does not hear the cries of distress of his daughters – even those not yet knowing they are loved by the Lord.

Hagar was to return to her boss, but she did so now in a relationship with the Lord. She was now, in the Lord's eyes, not below Sarai and not above her, but rather alongside. This is equality in the Lord's eyes – he has no favourites. Even if her position of employment was different, she was equally loved.

Sarai would not respond as harshly to someone who no longer showed her contempt, and in time, of course, Sarai's story was going to include a physical miracle as the worn-out woman (her words[4]) conceived and carried to full term the real heir of destiny. But now, as Hagar returned to her mistress, the war was over! The one who started it, by letting contempt fester, ended it!

Before we end this chapter let's make this personal. Have you, like Hagar, wanted to run away from a difficult relationship and found yourself in a wilderness experience as a result? Have you felt so misunderstood that you mentally dress-rehearse your case to defend your position and pain? I want to encourage you today to know that there is no wilderness, no hiding place and no hurt which prevents the Lord from seeing you. Like Hagar, you are seen. Like Hagar, you are loved. Like Hagar, your story is not finished yet!

9

Holiness, not holey-ness

Let's revisit briefly the story of Hagar and Sarai. Until her personal encounter with the Lord in the wilderness, Hagar's relationship with God was not mentioned. Her position with her owners would have aligned her with some behavioural practices, but transformation by the Lord's love needs to be a personal experience. Hagar's work was also her life.

When I was a child my parents owned and managed their own hotel. Their hotel was our family home too. So the context of my upbringing was that there was blending between home and work. My mum always brought her work home with her – because she was already home. She did not have the option of compartmentalizing her work and home life. But perhaps this great challenge was in fact a great opportunity. Like my mum's, Hagar's work and home life also completely overlapped and as such were both transformed when she had her encounter with the Lord. Perhaps there are too many times when we work and live keeping a secular and sacred divide, such that knowing Christ makes no difference to our work life. Instead of considering compartmentalizing work and home, perhaps we would all benefit from a more holistic view of life. A friend once admitted to me that, after a decade working in the same job, none of her colleagues knew about her faith. Preaching is not necessary at work (although in fairness it is in mine!) but how we work should be consistent with our beliefs.

Jesus taught his followers that they were to be distinctive, to stand out, and that they were to be known for their good works – not for the sake of their own reputation but for the sake of God's!

You are the salt of the earth. But what good is salt if it has lost its flavour? Can you make it salty again? It will be thrown out and trampled underfoot as worthless.

You are the light of the world – like a city on a hilltop that cannot be hidden. No one lights a lamp and then puts it under a basket. Instead, a lamp is placed on a stand, where it gives light to everyone in the house. In the same way, let your good deeds shine out for all to see, so that everyone will praise your heavenly Father. (Matthew 5.13–16)

If you work in a secular context, do you carry the very essence of Christ into your workplace? Or if you work in a Christian context, do your friends and family see the same person your colleagues see when it comes to your behaviour, your movie choices, your drinking habits and as you relax?

For Hagar, when she met with God, *everything* changed! In this page-turning battle between these two women, once Hagar had encountered the Lord for herself their combined narrative changed. No reference to Sarai and Hagar's relationship is made after Hagar's encounter with the Lord in the wilderness: there was nothing of note to report! No drama. No animosity. No jealousy, contempt or harsh treatment. Instead the 'logs' and 'specks' were dealt with and they got on with their lives.

Sarai overheard a conversation and in doing so received a promise from the Lord. Sarai became Sarah. With her new name Sarah received her new identity as the 'mother of nations' even before she had conceived a child.[1] Sarah was blessed richly, favoured as a mother to many nations, giving birth to kings. There would be no threat from Hagar. She was free to be who she was created to be. And isn't that something we all deeply desire for ourselves and also for the women around us?

Contempt is like a needle digging into your spirit that seeks out the rubbish in your heart and draws it to the surface. That's fine if it's a refining process being handled by the Lord, but terrible if it is simply a magnet for relational chaos. It is so hard to lovingly, carefully lead someone on your team who holds you in contempt simply because you are in leadership! The pull to treat them harshly is so strong. Yet by the grace of God no stone needs to be thrown. It is possible to allow the junk that surfaces in the pull of contempt to be handed over to the Lord, not dumped on your co-worker.

Working with Hagar after her wilderness experience, when she knew that she was heard, seen, loved and released, was apparently much easier than working with Hagar before that moment of transformation.

What about our moments of transformation? Are we an easier employee when we know we are loved, seen and heard by the Lord? Does our walk with the Lord affect our work with women?

Do we need to hear the loving question of the Lord come to us to remind us and challenge us: 'Where have you come from and where are you going?'

If you are an employee – have you ever held your boss in contempt? Do you think you could do the boss's job better than he or she does, but for some reason have not had the opportunity? Are you on the receiving end of harsh treatment? Do you know the Lord hears and sees you? He loves your strengths and he knows your weaknesses. Can you allow the Lord to help you soften your heart – work hard and work fair – and deal with your biases?

If you are a boss – do you have a Hagar in your team? Does her contempt cause you to treat her harshly? Do you know that the Lord hears and sees you? He loves your strength and he knows your weaknesses. Can you allow the Lord to help you soften your heart – work hard and work fair – and deal with your biases?

I love hearing stories and have thoroughly enjoyed chatting with many friends about their working experience. While all their names have been changed, their stories haven't.

Sonia has been my friend for over three decades. She is a capable, intelligent woman working for a transnational consumer goods company. She has a brilliant brain for maths and problem-solving, is focused and hard-working and, as a result, has worked her way up some significant rungs in the corporate ladder. She has worked with four female bosses and, in her words, 'all except one were disastrous, controlling and with no trust!' Sonia went on to say that the lady boss who was great to work with was 'like one of the boys, so was enjoyable to work for!' Sonia's experience confirms the narrative to her that the female nature is to be controlling. She believes that 'in the corporate world, women still have to work harder to be as successful as the men. Women compete with each other – it is human nature – survival of the fittest.' Sonia's relationship with the Lord shapes her more than her experiences with 'disastrous' bosses and has compelled her to be different, to keep her heart soft. To allow her love for the Lord to be translated into her professional and personal relationships, Sonia has determined that she won't seek to control others and will intentionally choose to trust team members. There might never be an opportunity to share her faith with words (although Sonia is open to this) but there is every opportunity to share her faith through good work.

In contrast to Sonia's experience, my friend Alexandra has always favoured female bosses. Alexandra has worked in the spheres of social care and education, where the workforce has been predominantly female. Alexandra concludes that women who can't get on with other women must 'feel insecure or threatened – maybe there is no one to flirt with or pull the wool over the eyes with – such as taking time off for "women's problems"' – which she feels is an excuse women would not tolerate but men would. This makes it sound a potentially harder working environment if women are not compassionate with each other, but in her experience Alexandra finds a female-dominated work environment to be a more authentic, transparent workplace.

Another one of my friends, Anna, is a young woman whose challenge at work is more connected with finding her comfort zone on the spectrum of womanhood, which we discussed earlier. Like many, she is already accruing a number of career changes and has recently moved from education into the prison service. Anna describes herself as 'not the most feminine person' so felt she 'stuck out like a sore thumb among the teachers, where the school was dominated by women. However, I blend in very well with the female prison officers', who in her observation are working in a very masculine environment. Anna felt the pressure in teaching to negotiate successfully the tension of being both tough and feminine. However, in the environment of the prison there is a greater freedom – freedom in the sense of not being under pressure to be overtly 'feminine', and describing her 'wonderful' female colleagues as 'quite masculine'.

Later we will look more deeply into how we can become truly authentic to who we are, but in the meantime the challenge remains: can we bring our whole selves to work such that the Father's love is seen through us?

When women work together for the bettering of others, there can be a powerful transformation in a workplace. There's a tiny story tucked away in the book of Exodus about two midwives who work together under a huge amount of pressure from the authorities. They don't get the opportunity to testify specifically to the Lord's love, but they model something through their work that literally saves a generation of boys!

The story of Shiphrah and Puah is set in Egypt. The legacy of jealousy from the 'sisters at war' that we looked at in Chapter 3 continued in the jealousy that their sons felt towards each other. The target of the jealousy was Rachel's first biological son, Joseph. Such was the animosity towards Joseph that his brothers threw him into a pit before deciding to sell him into slavery. This began a cascading season of trials before eventual restoration in Egypt. Joseph, after surviving the pit, slavery and prison, ended up being promoted second only to the Pharaoh in power and eventually moved all his family to be with him in Egypt, forgiving his brothers in the process. Eventually Joseph and all his brothers died, but by then there were many descendants and they continued to grow in number and in strength. However, years passed and 'a new king came to power in Egypt who knew nothing about Joseph or what he had done' (Exodus 1.8). Fear gripped this king because he felt outnumbered.

> He said to his people, 'Look, the people of Israel now outnumber us and are stronger than we are. We must make a plan to keep them from growing even more. If we don't, and if war breaks out, they will join our enemies and fight against us. Then they will escape from the country.'
>
> So the Egyptians made the Israelites their slaves. They appointed brutal slave drivers over them, hoping to wear them down with crushing labour.
> (Exodus 1.9–11)

The more oppression the Egyptians piled on to the Israelites, the more strength and numbers the Israelites seemed to gain. So the Pharaoh concocted a wicked and ruthless plan that if he couldn't destroy the Israelites through hard labour he would destroy them at source and make their first breath their last breath! He demanded that Shiphrah and Puah, the two Hebrew midwives who looked after all the Hebrew women, watch as the Hebrew women gave birth and ensure that every baby boy born would be killed.

Up until this point Shiphrah and Puah's midwifery work would have been conducted unnoticed; however, suddenly the Egyptian masters were watching. Without compromising their love for the Lord, their work must have suddenly seemed impossible. But these midwives knew that whoever they worked for at a human level, God was more important, and *how* they worked was essential. They didn't keep their faith limited to home but allowed it to infiltrate every sphere of their life. Shiphrah and Puah concocted a shrewd plan.

> But because the midwives feared God, they refused to obey the king's orders. They allowed the boys to live, too.
> So the king of Egypt called for the midwives. 'Why have you done this?' he demanded. 'Why have you allowed the boys to live?'
> 'The Hebrew women are not like the Egyptian women,' the midwives replied. 'They are more vigorous and have their babies so quickly that we cannot get there in time.'
> So God was good to the midwives, and the Israelites continued to multiply, growing more and more powerful. And because the midwives feared God, he gave them families of their own.
> (Exodus 1.17–21)

What courageous, Spirit-filled women they were to know that what they did in the Lord's eyes mattered more than what they were seen to do by Pharaoh. Loving and respecting the Lord more than they feared Pharaoh, they embarked on an act of civil disobedience. But notice how they explain the babies' survival rates – they credit the Hebrew women as being strong. They don't finger-point or blame other women to justify their own decisions not to do something that is bad in the Lord's eyes. Instead, they credit the other women along the way. They don't save their necks by standing on anyone else's. They honour, affirm and protect the new mums – affirming their strength, championing their abilities, protecting the women and their babies.

You might have bosses who seem impossible and you might not be able to imagine how your life's good works can demonstrate the Father's love to your colleagues and your boss. You might work in an environment where you are on high alert all the time. My encouragement to you is to look at how Paul encouraged Timothy. Paul recognized the significant challenge that exists in trying to do right by those in authority – yet the most significant of responses is not in blind obedience but rather in humble prayer.

> Pray this way for kings and all who are in authority so that we can live peaceful and quiet lives marked by godliness and dignity. This is good and pleases God our Saviour, who wants everyone to be saved and to understand the truth. For,
>> There is one God and one Mediator who can reconcile God and humanity – the man Christ Jesus. He gave his life to purchase freedom for everyone.
>
> (1 Timothy 2.2–6)

I heard someone share once that they made sure they got to work earlier than any of their colleagues in order to be able to walk around the office and pray over every work station. Work at *whatever* you do as if for the Lord.

10

Wear the uniform

Just like my own kids, I had a school uniform which I moaned about and wore under duress. The grey skirt, white shirt and pink (yes pink – visualize musty-cerise rather than baby, if that helps!) blazer set off 'perfectly' with the striped tie. I moaned because I didn't like it – who would? Yet at the same time I was grateful because there was no pressure to justify personal choice every day. It's fine to hate uniforms because we can blame someone else for having to wear them. Of course, in an attempt to express uniqueness and not conform to the uniform, I (like all the girls) would roll the skirt at the waistband and conform to the unwritten uniform rule-book issued by the students! It left the mufti days, when the uniform could be exchanged for your own clothes, as exceptional and highly treasured yet tension-inducing occasions! Mufti days, which I've observed as a parent too, can bring huge peaks in stress levels as that outfit needs to be perfect – looking as if you've thrown it together without so much as a thought *without* making you look as if you've thrown it together without so much as a thought!

Workplace uniforms can have a similar freedom, reducing the need to think, choose, spend and plan. Having a uniform can clarify the expectations. It takes away pressure. It enables alignment – remember those teacher briefings before school excursions to remind you that 'when you are in your uniform you are representing the school, so therefore behave worthy of it!'

Workplace uniforms have the potential to show rank and role before any personal introductions are made. The uniform makes the announcement itself.

In 2016 Nicola Thorp kicked against wearing a work 'uniform' when she was sent home from work for refusing to wear high heels.[1] Choosing to wear flat-blacks, or to present a face without make-up, was against the company rules of PricewaterhouseCoopers and she was sent home. But she didn't go before pointing out the sexist nature of the clothing rule, where a made-up face is arguably to help assist someone's appearance but not her skills, and heels increase the leg-line but not the accuracy of accountancy or professional aptitude.

Sadly, a year later the government rejected the claims that it was sexist, siding with the company's view that they could insist women wear high heels if it was part of the job description and that men were to dress with the same level of smartness (if not with the same heel-height).[2]

For us, as women in the workplace, is there a uniform available that announces something of alignments before we even need to speak? I don't mean we should all don a little fishy lapel badge, but something far more significant.

Simon Ward, a friend of mine who's also a leading voice among the British Fashion Council, once told me that he would always encourage women to dress not to *impress* but rather to *express*! Is there something we can wear to express something in the workplace that will also transform how we work?

As we saw in Chapter 5, Paul wrote about the armour of God, and it is clearly not something to be worn to impress rather than to express who we are in Christ.

So let's consider our working relationships with other women and what might change if, underneath all of our visible clothes, we first put on this spiritual kit list. If a belt is the essential item that holds everything in the middle together – stops things coming adrift at the wrong moment – then a belt of truth holding in place the body armour of God's righteousness would surely be helpful. Just imagine being so held together by truth and righteousness that we would be protected from getting caught up in lies, gossip and misrepresentations.

Before Paul talked about the armour of God he was encouraging the believers in Ephesus to allow all the gifts within the church to work together for the greater good of the Lord's purposes. So that

Then we will no longer be immature like children. We won't be tossed and blown about by every wind of new teaching. We will not be influenced when people try to trick us with lies so clever they sound like the truth. Instead, we will speak the truth in love, growing in every way more and more like Christ, who is the head of his body, the church. He makes the whole body fit together perfectly. As each part does its own special work, it helps the other parts grow, so that the whole body is healthy and growing and full of love.
(Ephesians 4.14–16)

'Girding ourselves' prevents us from being tossed around by clever arguments and will enable us to be confident in truth and to speak in the love that the Lord enables us to know. The partnership between truth and love is essential. Truth without love can lead to legalism; however, love without truth can lead to being led by fickle feelings.

Today truth is diluted by relativism, the 'doctrine' that there are no absolute truths. It is held that truth is always relative to some particular frame of reference, such as a language or a culture. However, the gospel – if it is good news for everyone – must reach beyond language and culture. The gospel surely has to be as relevant for me in my suburban terrace as it does for my friend Grace in Malaysia or Zola living in the tents among the Syrian refugees in Lebanon – truth that transcends culture and language, beyond our upbringing, beyond our bias. The truth of Christ is absolute, life-giving and love-given.

Surely this is what Jesus was referring to when he encouraged his disciples to press into him, saying, 'You are truly my disciples if you remain faithful to my teachings. And you will know the truth, and the truth will set you free' (John 8.31–32). The truth here is a lived-out faith.

Being held together by truth will set us free from the grip of any comparison trap and from jealousy. Christ's truth will tell us what we need to know about the Father, about ourselves and about other women. In his truth there will be no need to compete negatively or be jealous.

Perceptions are relative, truth is absolute. We place high value on our feelings and credit our perceptions with great authority. We can become convinced by feelings and perceptions that Paul referred to as 'lies that are so clever that they sound like the truth'.[3] We can deceive ourselves as well as other people with great arguments and clever words, being misguided into thinking we are holding to truth when often we are not.

Again, let's gently remind ourselves that, in Jesus, truth is always packaged in love. Holding to absolute truth is not the same as holding to legalism, because only one requires love. As Jesus said in John's Gospel, 'I am the way, the truth, and the life. No one can come to the Father except through me' (John 14.6), showing that Truth is the person of Christ.

So if our core is held together by this beautiful belt of truth, what about what's on our feet? Let's consider the shoes of peace. You will have heard it said that you shouldn't judge someone until you have walked a mile in their shoes. Of course, this is not gospel – because even if we'd walked ten miles in someone's shoes the Lord doesn't invite us to judge them. However, he does invite us to walk in peace – to assume the best of those around us – to daily walk putting grace before hypocrisy and forgiveness before the fight. To walk in peace, becoming the person where gossip always stops. To be ready in every season to share the good news of Christ with every step that we take.

The shield of faith is designed to combat arrows from the enemy rather than for clubbing your co-workers around their heads when conflict arises. To be defended against the enemy's fiery arrows we must first recognize who the enemy is and then confidently hold faith in front of us in defence as we move forward. This is a striking image of soldiers in full armour standing shoulder to shoulder with shields locked together, creating an impenetrable barrier. There is a power and strength that comes from women putting their shields of faith alongside those of others for combined strength and protection, when our defences are not against each other but with each other and against our spiritual enemy.

The prophet Isaiah declared:

But in that coming day no weapon turned against you will succeed. You will silence every voice raised up to accuse you. These benefits are enjoyed by the servants of the LORD; their vindication will come from me. I, the LORD, have spoken! (Isaiah 54.17)

Of course there are going to be weapons formed against us. Of course there are going to be challenges – but just imagine how different things could be if together we held impenetrable shields of faith-in-him around us, defended to the hilt by him.

Many women spend a lot of time considering their appearance, not only so that they feel good about themselves, not to attract a mate, but rather to impress women around them. The fear of the awkwardness that can arise when two women turn up at an event wearing the same outfit induced my daughter's class to check out their prom dresses with each other before the big day. Two girls didn't check in advance and actually ended up wearing the same outfit. Instead of celebrating each other's great taste in clothes they were awkward, embarrassed and sadly the subject of some post-prom ridicule.

A friend of mine is a lawyer – a wig-and-robe-wearing lawyer – who tells me she feels that the putting on of the uniform is an empowering moment in comparison to those around her. It provides her with a sense of equality with her peers, superiority over defendants and authority with her clients. All that from one robe and wig. Wigs and gowns are not accessories in my workplace, and probably not in yours either. However, we've all dressed to give a specific impression on occasions, in comparison to those around us.

The wonder of the armour of God is that it equips us from the inside out! The power is not in the comparison of our outer appearance but rather in the presence of the Holy Spirit within us.

The Gospels tell how Jesus was crucified. His dead body was wrapped in cloth and buried in the grave. After three days, as Jesus came back to life he left the grave behind him, along with the unnecessary linen wrappings.[4] The cloth that was needed in death was no longer required in his resurrected life.

The pressure of dressing to impress keeps us trapped by comparisons in our relationships. As we escape the comparison trap we no longer need to dress to impress, compete or prove our identity. There is a better season ahead for us of freedom in Christ – far from the prison of other people's opinions about us.

So, friend – what are you wearing to work this week?

Part 3

INNER BATTLES

UNDER BATTLE

11

Do you belong here?

We've seen that there are challenges in the relationships we have with other women in various contexts and especially at work. But there is another battleground for women that is also highly contested – the battle with ourselves! In this section we're going to get *really* personal! Let me kick this off with a story.

A simple 'hello' would have sufficed but I offered, 'Hi, I'm a gate-crasher!' by means of introduction to the charity director sitting next to me. I was trying to stay under the radar and attend this presentation without really being noticed, but this 'greet your neighbour' moment proved a challenge. A global corporation was launching some fresh opportunities for partnerships with pre-approved community initiatives as part of their global goals. I was new to the conversations and not officially on the partnership list, but I'd been invited to come and hear a little bit more. It was possible that, in time, a project I was seeking to launch might be added to this list of partners and would benefit from the volunteer wisdom, expertise and time of some of these global corporation employees. But my idea was embryonic and I was not sure I really belonged. So introducing myself as a mere gate-crasher was my apologetic 'hello'.

'Impostor syndrome' is a term that was coined by clinical psychologists Pauline Clance and Suzanne Imes in 1978 when they found that, despite having adequate external evidence of accomplishments, many people remain convinced they don't deserve the success they have.

It is the inner voice that insists, 'You don't belong here.' It is the voice that says, 'You will be found out to be a fraud soon.' It is your inner voice that becomes a weapon against you, fuelling an inner war.

In her book *Becoming*, Michelle Obama writes that there was

the doubt that sat in my mind through student orientation, through my first sessions of high school biology and English, through my somewhat fumbling get-to-know-you conversations in the cafeteria with new friends. *Not enough. Not enough.* It was doubt about where I came from and what I'd believed about myself until now. It was like a malignant cell that threatened to divide and divide again, unless I could find some way to stop it.[1]

Negative thoughts, as we have noted, have a huge capacity to multiply. Truth sounds more doubtful and doubts more truthful. Our minds would be spared a lot of stress from negative over-thinking if we would learn to doubt our doubts!

Impostor syndrome has an impact on many women every day. You probably know how it goes. You get a good grade in school and you think that there must have been some favourable grade boundaries. You get the promotion at work and you think you must have been the only candidate. You are asked to speak at that event and the inner story in your head says you are being asked because everyone else must have been busy. You are sitting in a meeting and you are just waiting for your boss to turn round and ask you to leave because she's finally realized you're not qualified. Or you have to do a presentation for your studies and your inner narrative says that your classmates are finally going to realize what a loser you are and will assume that you must have cheated in your coursework and credits to date.

Impostor syndrome traps us in insecurity which can lead us to feel defensive or hypersensitive because we feel vulnerable. In turn, this vulnerability can be exploited by competitive women, which can accentuate our insecurity and keep us trapped in comparison. It can become a self-perpetuating cycle.

This private you-against-you war can derail you before you begin your life journey. Don't become your own enemy and allow yourself to self-sabotage your own future.

The Gospels record the story of a woman who had reached the end of her capacity to cope with the personal war she was enduring, and the way she reached out in an all-or-nothing hope. For 12 years this woman had endured significant gynaecological challenges.[2] Because she was still bleeding, in a sustained period, we know that she was pre-menopause. Even if she had a few days' reprieve she clearly did not pass the Levitical law requirement of not bleeding for seven days, because she remained unclean for 12 years! So it must be that even if she had six days without bleeding she never had longer than that during the 12-year 'unclean' time. According to Levitical law, she was unclean[3] and as a result would have been isolated and ostracized to prevent her from 'contaminating' others.

The months bled into a long period of suffering. She put as many resources as she had at her disposal to try and get medical support and fix her problem – but nothing helped.

Jesus was on his way to Jairus' house because Jairus' daughter was dying. A crowd had gathered around Jesus and Jairus, no doubt keen to see what was going to take place. The accounts of miracles accompanied Jesus so he rarely walked alone. The shoving and jostling crowd was penetrated by a brave and desperate woman – bent over in pain and brokenness, she weaved through the crowd to reach out to Jesus.It is popularly said that she reached out to touch the hem of Jesus' garment: 'Coming up behind Jesus, she touched the fringe of his robe' (Luke 8.44).

The 'fringe' that was touched would most likely have been on the *tallit*, or prayer shawl, that Jesus wore. Tied to each of the four corners of the *tallit* that Jewish men wore were tassels called *tzitziyot*. These tassels served to remind each Jewish man of his responsibility to obey God's commandments and fulfil his obligation to the law. 'These tassels are tied into 613 knots to constantly remind them of the 613 laws of Moses, of which there are 365 prohibitions (the "thou shalt not" laws), and 248 affirmations (the "thou shall" laws).'[4] The shawl was draped to be visible as the outer garment, symbolically showing everyone that the man was walking in the way of the Lord's law. In fact, the Hebrew word we translate as 'law' is *halacha*, which literally means 'walk'.[5] Jesus was wearing clothes that expressed his commitment to walk in the way of the law of the Lord, and in this story the woman who was, according to that law, unclean reached out and touched the very part of his robe that was linked to the law. At this exact point, legally speaking, this woman made Jesus unclean. However, something else was experienced by the woman and by Jesus!

> Coming up behind Jesus, she touched the fringe of his robe. Immediately, the bleeding stopped.
>
> 'Who touched me?' Jesus asked.
>
> Everyone denied it, and Peter said, 'Master, this whole crowd is pressing up against you.'
>
> But Jesus said, 'Someone deliberately touched me, for I felt healing power go out from me.' When the woman realized that she could not stay hidden, she began to tremble and fell to her knees in front of him. The whole crowd heard her explain why she had touched him and that she had been immediately healed.
>
> (Luke 8.44–47)

Instead of the uncleanness going from the woman to Jesus, it was his power that went to her. Her desperate desire to see an end to her physical, emotional and spiritual battle caused her to reach out in faith, and Jesus' power went to her, healing her. This was not just a physical healing. This would reconnect her with family and friends.

She would be able to touch and be touched, sleep on a mattress, remain in her family home, connect with her community.

Furthermore, the inner voice that would have raged within this woman telling her she was an outsider – did not belong, was not worthy to receive love, had no value, was an impostor, was unclean – finally met more than its match in the love of Jesus.

Turning to her, with compassion, the God–man who walked in the way of heaven's law to see it fulfilled declared over her, 'Daughter, your faith has made you well. Go in peace' (Luke 8.48).

This is the first time in Luke's Gospel that Jesus referred to a woman as 'daughter'. She belonged! She belonged, and peace was declared in her 'war zone'. First he affirmed that she belonged, as daughter, and then he declared her healed, in response to her faith. Jesus liberated her.

When we are willing to come as we are, with no pretence, no hiding, and to reach out to Jesus, then we too can be on the receiving end of his compassionate, loving power. As we come into relationship and recognize to whom we belong, then we will discover the power that comes *from* him in response to our faith *in* him. The inner voice that tells us we don't belong can be silenced. Whether it is physical, emotional, mental or spiritual suffering, in response to his love, compassion and power we too can discover healing. In his plans we need not feel like an impostor.

Jesus wants you to receive his power. He is not choosing to withhold but waiting to impart, as he promised, 'you will receive power when the Holy Spirit comes upon you' (Acts 1.8). Now is as good a time as any to reach out!

The book of Acts describes a turning point in the advancement of the gospel when Peter recognized that the Lord had not come just for the Jews but also for the Gentiles. In a graphic vision he saw a sheet lowered from heaven containing all sorts of animals, reptiles and birds. He then heard a voice telling him to eat. This was an outrageous and abhorrent instruction because Peter had been schooled and conditioned to only eat certain meat and never touch anything deemed impure or unclean according to the Levitical law. However – three times this message was repeated. On conclusion of the vision, it wasn't Peter's diet that was changed as much as his mission. The message of the gospel went to those who were previously understood to be 'unclean'. 'But the voice spoke again: "Do not call something unclean if God has made it clean"' (Acts 10.15).

Just as Peter learned a powerful lesson and the woman-no-longer-bleeding realized that she had been made clean and belonged, so too can we come to the turning point of understanding that we must not call unclean what God has called clean.

The voice may continue to tell us we are merely gate-crashers to this event, we don't fit in, we don't belong – but if God has declared us clean and positioned us for purpose let's allow his power and peace to infiltrate us and declare a ceasefire. Let him set you free.

Imagine as you stand in front of the mirror and declare truths about yourself – don't call unclean what God has called clean! Don't call ugly what he calls beautiful. Don't call stupid what he calls marvellous. Don't call ridiculous what he calls wonderfully complex.

You made all the delicate, inner parts of my body
    and knit me together in my mother's womb.
Thank you for making me so wonderfully complex!
    Your workmanship is marvellous – how well I know it.
You watched me as I was being formed in utter seclusion,
    as I was woven together in the dark of the womb.
You saw me before I was born.
    Every day of my life was recorded in your book.
Every moment was laid out
    before a single day had passed.
How precious are your thoughts about me, O God.
    They cannot be numbered!

I can't even count them;
    they outnumber the grains of sand!
And when I wake up,
    you are still with me!
(Psalm 139.13–18)

You are loved, you are known, you are positioned for purpose –
you belong here! He sees your frame, your form, he knows your
heart and mind and has nothing but precious thoughts towards you.
He sees your comings and goings as you work, rest, play, whether in
the company of many or on your own.

He is glad that you are part of the beautiful wonder that is
womanhood. He is glad you are incomparable, unique and beautifully you. It is not a mistake that you were created as a woman, but a
divine plan to demonstrate his glory through you.

He knows the dreams you have and the hopes no human ear has
heard – he hears. He is positioning you for a purpose that might
even go beyond your imagination – he sees your destiny clearly. His
plans are good. His intentions towards you are good. He is loving.
He only gives good gifts.

That range of emotions that makes you feel you are crazy is a
beautiful reflection of the wonderfully complex woman that you are.
He loves the breadth and depth of your passions and thoughts. He
made you with a huge capacity to feel and think. He's also equipped
you not to be controlled by this range of feelings but to be set free
with his truth.

Even when it feels as though there is a crowd jostling around, or
so much commotion it's as if Jesus keeps disappearing from your
view, he is there – he knows when you reach out to him and he is
ready to respond to you. His power will be made real in you because
you are his daughter.

His power and his peace are available for you if you will reach
out and receive, enabling the inner battle that pops up within

you – or the full-on war that is your constant experience – to be silenced, your enemies defeated, the ceasefire declared and peace-time enjoyed.

You are not out of place in his purposes because you are positioned in his family, so remain in his love, remain 'belonging' – he will direct your path.

12

Hush

As we continue to challenge our inner battler, let's consider some of the triggers and influences we have to deal with which affect how we relate to other women around us.

The psalmist advocates that choosing how we are influenced will enable us to be effective in all seasons. *The Message* paraphrases this brilliantly:

> How well God must like you –
>   you don't hang out at Sin Saloon,
>   you don't slink along Dead-End Road,
>   you don't go to Smart-Mouth College.
> Instead you thrill to GOD's Word,
>   you chew on Scripture day and night.
> You're a tree replanted in Eden,
>   bearing fresh fruit every month,
> never dropping a leaf,
>   always in blossom.
> (Psalm 1.1–3, *The Message*)

Choosing to 'thrill to GOD's Word' and having a daily discipline of reading his truth is a life-changing habit to develop. Because, whether we do this or not, we are on the receiving end of a constant bombardment of influences.

Digital marketing experts estimate that most Americans are exposed to between 4,000 and 10,000 advertisements each day. 'Through mobile phones, online entertainment services, the Internet, electronic mail, television, radio, newspapers, books, social media etc. people receive every day about 105,000 words or 23 words per second in half a day (12 hours) (during awake hours).'[1]

Digital billboards and posters might accompany commuters in their peripheral vision but hand-held devices provide a more constant source of information.

Over ten years ago *The Guardian* reported:

> In one 45-minute journey, the average London commuter is exposed to more than 130 adverts, featuring more than 80 different products. Only half of that information makes any impact, while unprompted we can remember none of the blur of adverts. In an entire day, we're likely to see 3,500 marketing messages.[2]

It is widely reported that 'businesses make an average of $2 in revenue for every $1 they spend on Google Ads'.[3]

If our passive engagement with various methods of media advertising can have such a profitable outcome for the Google advertiser, how much more influence might media have when we are actively engaged, such as watching a film or television show or listening to music?

When was the last time you switched off a song, a film or a programme because it was having a negative impact, an unhelpful influence, on your mind? When was the last time you actively personally policed the media you allow yourself to be exposed to? I don't mean that awkward moment when your dad fast-forwarded the film to avoid that content or your mum told you to look away but, rather, when did you personally take responsibility for the messages that passively and intentionally infiltrate your thoughts?

Personal discontentment, interpersonal jealousies and comparison traps can increase with unscrutinized media exposure.

Satisfying the appetite to delve into someone else's life through magazine stories, reality shows and gossip games will influence not only how we perceive other people but also how we perceive ourselves.

In his letter to the Corinthians Paul urged the Christ-followers to be vigilant and not succumb to cultural mindsets and false arguments. Again, recognizing their battles were actually at a spiritual level rather than with a specific person, he urged them to 'destroy every proud obstacle that keeps people from knowing God. We capture their rebellious thoughts and teach them to obey Christ' (2 Corinthians 10.5).

A rebellious thought can be understood to be a thought which is not in line with the thinking of Christ. So let's take a moment to get really personal – when was the last time you made any attempt to capture any rebellious thoughts that you had to make them obedient to Christ?

The Message paraphrase says this well:

the world is unprincipled. It's dog-eat-dog out there! The world doesn't fight fair. But we don't live or fight our battles that way – never have and never will. The tools of our trade aren't for marketing or manipulation, but they are for demolishing that entire massively corrupt culture. We use our powerful God-tools for smashing warped philosophies, tearing down barriers erected against the truth of God, fitting every loose thought and emotion and impulse into the structure of life shaped by Christ. Our tools are ready at hand for clearing the ground of every obstruction and building lives of obedience into maturity.

(2 Corinthians 10.3–6, *The Message*)

Imagine for a moment that you are a powerlifter with super-strength and the additional bonus of great cardiovascular health and agility. In fact, go ahead, just imagine for a moment that you are a superhero! You have had a peaceful evening at home, enjoyed a delicious meal and are now upstairs resting. Just as you are nodding off you hear the sound of breaking glass and realize there is an intruder breaking into your home. What do you do?

Maybe you will quietly investigate the whereabouts, capacity and strength of the intruder. On discovering that he or she isn't nearly as strong or agile as you, wouldn't you apprehend, interrupt or chase off the burglar?

So, if that is what we would do in our homes, should we not be protecting our minds just as much? Of course, none of us actually have superpowers – but in Jesus we have a supernatural God, who is both human and God. That is as much superpower as we will ever need against our spiritual enemies!

James wrote, 'resist the devil, and he will flee from you. Come close to God, and he will come close to you' (James 4.7–8). It is time for a revolution in our thinking. It is time to take back control of our thinking, take our enemies captive and surrender our minds to Christ.

Neuroscientist Dr Caroline Leaf wrote:

> The average person has over 30,000 thoughts a day. Through an uncontrolled thought life, we create the conditions for illness; we make ourselves sick! Research shows that fear, all on its own, triggers more than 1,400 known physical and chemical responses and activates more than 30 different hormones . . . Consciously controlling your thought life means not letting thoughts rampage through your mind. It means learning to engage interactively with every single thought that you have, and to analyse it before you decide either to accept or reject it.[4]

I love the way science is catching up with the biblical wisdom that we need to restrict the movement of our thoughts and allow them to be scrutinized for our well-being.

As we take control of negative thoughts we will silence our enemies. In the context of that silence we can ready ourselves for encountering the Lord.

In Chapter 9, when we were looking at how women can experience conflict with each other in the workplace I asked the question, 'If you work in a Christian context, do your friends and family see the same person your colleagues see when it comes to your movie choices . . .?' Whatever sphere you work in, do you put any checks and balances in place for the media messages you might allow to influence you?

Many years ago my husband and I made the personal decision to avoid watching films that were rated '18'. Obviously it's not because we're too young, but rather we wanted to guard our thinking. We decided that we didn't need to see things that we might want to 'unsee' later. We've made an occasional exception, but this practice has helped us, and by blocking out a few films we've not missed out at all. But am I as selective in putting down the magazine that presents all the gorgeous homes some women live in or turning away from the pictures of the famous looking fabulous when I find them fuelling my discontent and harbouring negative thoughts towards others? Do I close the magazine that celebrates the candid, unguarded shots of celebrity women because the paparazzi somehow make me feel better about myself when I compare myself to those photos? What feeds my mind can affect my ability to see my real disposition.

Perhaps now is the time for us to wake up and realize we're too often caught in the comparison trap. If so, there is hope to escape it, and in our busy, fast-paced, noisy contexts we can begin by establishing some guards around our minds.

In Psalm 46 David celebrates a God-enabled victory while at the same time speaking to silence his enemies so that they will know the sovereignty of the Lord, who says, 'Be still, and know that I am God!' (Psalm 46.10).

This is a revolution that will enable us to escape the grip of jealousy. We too can silence the negative inner clamour and lean into the Father's love, to discover a deeper revelation of intimacy.

Jesus told a parable of a farmer scattering seed, which landed in four different terrains, resulting in four different outcomes. Seeds falling on the path were eaten by birds, seeds on the rocks died through lack of good soil, seeds falling on the thorns were choked of life. However, seed falling on good soil settled and thrived and went on to produce a bountiful harvest. Jesus gave a detailed explanation for the parable, showing the significance of thought-life to his disciples. Some words are heard and forgotten or crowded out by other voices:

> The seeds that fell among the thorns represent those who hear the message, but all too quickly the message is crowded out by the cares and riches and pleasures of this life. And so they never grow into maturity. And the seeds that fell on the good soil represent honest, good-hearted people who hear God's word, cling to it, and patiently produce a huge harvest.
> (Luke 8.14–15)

Recognizing and rejecting what is crowding out truth in our thinking and instead clinging to the truth of Christ will produce positive things in our life – mentally, physically and spiritually.

With hundreds of external media messages vying for our attention and thousands of thoughts taking place in our own minds, now is the time to recognize the power of Christ to help us find freedom, peace and the gift of silence.

> Don't copy the behaviour and customs of this world, but let God transform you into a new person by changing the way you think. Then you will learn to know God's will for you, which is good and pleasing and perfect.
> (Romans 12.2)

When it comes to victory in our thinking and the revolution of our renewed minds, the comparison trap between women must be addressed. The narrative must change that we are 'not . . . enough'. Not good enough, not smart enough, not fast enough, not strong enough, not old enough, not young enough, not thin enough, not female enough, not . . . enough!

By letting go of the way the world thinks while clinging tight to the word of Christ we can be transformed, renewed – and become all that God intends us to be.

Comparison is the thief who is comfortable robbing you of life in broad daylight! Comparison is the liar who will tease, taunt and try to use misappropriated stories against you. Comparison is the friend of the discontented and disappointed. Comparison is the enemy of gratitude. Comparison is the seed that multiplies its toxicity, coursing through a person's veins like a cancerous cell. Comparison needs to be taken captive and made obedient to Christ.

Dr Caroline Leaf said:

> Comparison is a killer, plain and simple. It will keep you focused on what is happening externally, and allow things to go amuck internally, which can impact both your mental and physical health. You can never be like someone else, because the law of the brain is diversity: there is no one way of doing life or dealing with a situation. If you try to be like or act like another person, you will make yourself more and more anxious because you are setting yourself up to fail.[5]

Later on we will look at what it means to be uniquely you, but today the inner battle needs to be recognized. The inner voice of comparison is not your friend but rather an impostor, an intruder that needs to be restricted and removed.

In contrast, Paul is raising the bar; he shows there is a way to fix our thoughts on all that is good, in such a way that we might discover a liberating motivation where we can compare ourselves to who the Lord intends us to be.

Paul wrote to the Philippians:

Fix your thoughts on what is true, and honourable, and right, and pure, and lovely, and admirable. Think about things that are excellent and worthy of praise. Keep putting into practice all you learned and received from me – everything you heard from me and saw me doing. Then the God of peace will be with you.

(Philippians 4.8–9)

It is time to discover God's presence, his voice and his truth – and above all, know that you are loved.

13

It's to be expected

As we continue to discover the increased freedom that is available to us as we overcome our inner battles, we're going to take a look at another biblical story. This is about the physical struggle one woman endures as a result of her pregnancy. Rebekah, wife of Isaac (daughter-in-law to Abraham and Sarah), apparently struggled to conceive – however, when she finally did become pregnant, after 20 years of marriage, the struggle took on a whole different dimension. 'The two children struggled with each other in her womb. So she went to ask the LORD about it. "Why is this happening to me?" she asked' (Genesis 25.22). I love the simplicity of this question – 'Why is this happening to me?' – and find myself wanting to respond, 'Because you are pregnant – what do you expect?' But with the absence of any ultrasound technology Rebekah had no way of understanding that she was pregnant with *two* babies until they were big enough to be felt from the outside of her belly or when they put in their first appearance. Having never been pregnant before, and unsure if she was definitely carrying twins, at times she would have found the sensations of two boys jostling for space within her womb really uncomfortable, maybe terrifying and even excruciating.

My friend Helen, who herself csarried twin boys, described it as feeling as if there were 'two gym classes going on inside'. Her scans proved that her boys were indeed 'kicking each other' until finally there were only 'squashed movements, as if they were pushing each other out of the way'. Yikes – imagine feeling all of that and not knowing why! No wonder Rebekah wondered what was happening to her.

What was happening to Rebekah, though, was entirely natural. Nothing was wrong with her. Hindsight would confirm all was okay. 'And when the time came to give birth, Rebekah discovered that she did indeed have twins!' (Genesis 25.24).

As we've seen before, the very thing that had been desired was now a source of great challenge, but this was particularly interesting because the baby-blessing was doubled!

We've explored what it is to have an inner conflict of battling right from wrong in our own minds. However, what happens when the conflict we experience is not so much about 'right from wrong' but rather 'best from good'?

I've personally experienced and observed the tension that so many women carry of wrestling between good things and trying to work out which thing or what person should take priority.

Several years ago I went away on a private retreat; my primary focus was to be alone with the Lord in order to progress my first 'book-baby' that I'd been carrying for a number of years. Life was getting in the way, constant distraction pulled me away from writing and the book-baby was being neglected. So I went away and spent some time in prayer, reading, studying and trying to write! The surprising challenge, though, was that as I was studying I felt a spiritual download happening in my spirit – a revelation of a thought which I immediately recognized as another 'book-baby'! Later in the day I rang my husband to update him on the progress of Book-baby 1 and shared my excitement of Book-baby 2. My excitement was not matched in any shape, size or form by my husband. His voice slowed and sank. We weren't on a video call, but I didn't need to see him to know that he was not looking happy! He urged me not to get distracted, to finish what I'd started. The challenge of completing Book-baby 1 would surely be exacerbated by being 'pregnant' with a whole new project! 'Keep focus, Helen,' he urged me lovingly.

But I couldn't now choose between them! I was carrying 'double revelation' and they were in some ways in opposition to each other; I was going to have to work out how to carry both to completion.

What if the wrestling within us is not about carrying two books or two babies like Rebekah's twins, Jacob and Esau? Just as Jacob grew up to be a stay-at-home sort of man and Esau was an out-and-about type guy, so we often have similar differences. As women, don't we often experience the home-and-away conflict?

These conflicts appear all over the place – the woman trying to care for children or elderly or sick relatives while also needing to hold down a job, the single parent who doesn't have the luxury of someone to provide tag-team support and has to shoulder everything, the student who needs to study to get the degree but at the same time needs to work to pay bills, the single person who longs to be in a loving relationship with someone more than her best mate or the cat but who, by the time she's home from work, is exhausted with no time to meet anyone!

You know that nagging shame-and-blame feeling that tells you that you are not doing enough – not working hard enough, not loving the family enough. As Rebekah needed the reassurance that everything was actually normal and okay, so do many of us!

As we read earlier, 'The temptations in your life are no different from what others experience. And God is faithful' (1 Corinthians 10.13).

In their book *What Would Boudicca Do?* Elizabeth Foley and Beth Coates have an unusual story to help us as their book celebrates 'everyday problems solved by history's most remarkable of women'.[1] These women write about a folk hero called Gráinne Ní Mháille, writing, 'Managing the obligations we owe to our jobs, friends and families is a delicate art. Who better to look to for advice on this sort of subtle, psychological challenge than a skirt-swirling, pistol-toting sixteenth-century pirate queen?'[2] Already a working mum with three girls,

in 1567 she also gave birth to their only son, Tiobóid, while on a sea voyage and under attack from Algerian pirates. In an admirable instance of work–life integration, and astonishing physical stamina, Gráinne inspired her troops by coming above deck wrapped in a blanket and brandishing a gun, just after producing the infant. For Gráinne work and family were always closely intertwined as her children fought with, and sometimes against her.[3]

Now, I'm not one to advocate a life of piracy (although my dad frequently boasts that a distant relative of ours was a pirate, so maybe, if there is a future career change for me, I should keep my options open!). But as Gráinne Ní Mháille discovered, when the enemies were climbing on board her ship and threatening her crew she was able to find the strength to fight, even with a newborn baby on her hip.

Perhaps I should remind you that I've still got Paul's teaching in mind – our fight is not against flesh and blood but in the spiritual realm. So our weapons can be directed towards the spiritual enemies – even with a baby on our hip or a book-baby in our hearts or an elderly relative needing our care and a job to be done!

As Foley and Coates encourage,

> Gráinne was expected to put all her energies into her home life but she found a balance that worked for her – one that led her into the commercial and martial sphere of men. However, she did not neglect the ties that bound her to her family and her community and, although few of us can look to a corsairing career on the open seas for fulfilment, we can feel good about following our own paths, against the expectations imposed upon us by others, and about balancing out our responsibilities with whatever floats our boats.[4]

Holding the tensions of the many demands we face in life can be an arduous and consuming inner conflict, a war with ourselves for trying to be all, do all and still having something left to give for the unexpected demands. These tensions have the capacity to pull us towards becoming people-pleasers.

Dr Caroline Leaf acknowledges the important difference between people motivated to be peacemakers and those who are people-pleasers. She says,

> A peace maker wants to restore balance and reach a resolution, and tries to see the issue from all sides in a rational and objective way. This person has a desire to help others; consequently, they will sometimes be willing to say the truth even if it hurts, and even if the people involved do not want to face reality. A people pleaser, however, is more self-focused and afraid of criticism. This person tends to be hypersensitive to uncertainty and conflict, and, as a result, will be more willing to sacrifice his or her values or mental health just to make someone else happy. This creates a toxic feedback loop: this person seeks approval because of their low self-confidence, which further lowers the value they place on themselves, and will weaken their resolve to stand up to people in the future. This can be quite dangerous; sometimes people who pick up on this desire to please can take advantage of the person in question, making them say and do things that go against their integrity.[5]

It is fascinating that the behavioural pattern of pleasing people stems from a 'self-focused' issue and feeds the need within. Dr Leaf continues,

> Essentially, being a people pleaser is a kind of survival instinct – we do it to avoid facing and dealing with our problems, which is a painful process . . . When you lie to yourself and are not true to who you are, you can experience an internal 'war' – what you say and do is not in agreement with what you

are thinking about or what you want. This can impact both your mental and physical health, because a lack of mental congruence drains your energy, causes toxic stress and affects the way information is processed and memory is built, which leads to neurochemical chaos in the brain and body.[6]

It's time for this private war to end, for us to stop being women turned against ourselves. The challenge to overcome this will be tough; however, I believe the path to our freedom from this inner war is easier than we might think – and definitely easier than our enemy wants us to believe!

Even if the juggling in your life is entirely of good things and the conflict is choosing best from good, there is a way through. Moving from trying to keep everybody happy, we're going to explore living for the many with an audience of one! We'll end the inner battle by having a one-centric focus influencing our purpose.

Rebekah realized what she experienced was actually normal – she gave birth to twins, one at a time! I found a way to write two books that were published at different times. Somehow pirate Gráinne Ní Mháille discovered she could fight with a baby on her hip!

The twin boys that Rebekah carried, who wrestled within her, came out and carried on wrestling into adult life. The boys competed with each other. The second-born, Jacob, stole Esau's birthright and blessing right from under his brother's nose.

Having come back from hunting, Esau prepared a meal for his father, expecting then to receive a significant blessing. However, he discovered too late that his brother Jacob had tricked his father into blessing him first. Devastated and furious, Esau implored his father to find a way around the restrictions and bless him as well.

The blessing that Esau received does not, at first glance, appear to be much of a blessing at all; however, there is one phrase that held keys for him – and might also be keys for us too, as we discover the freedom that comes when we live in every season as a Jesus-pleaser rather than a people-pleaser, as we learn to accept the challenges that overlap in the seasons we are in, as we learn to receive the strength that the Lord has for us and allow ourselves to rest when we're tired so we're strengthened to persevere.

Esau's blessing contained this phrase: 'when you decide to break free, you will shake his yoke from your neck' (Genesis 27.40). The power of deciding to break free from the battles that Esau experienced was in his hands; the timeline was his to decide.

What freedom might be yours to experience when you choose to be set free? What freedom might be yours when you choose no longer to listen to the blame-and-shame voice that says you are not enough, or not doing enough, as you try to care for your relatives and hold down your job at the same time? What freedom will come when you choose to be a Jesus-pleaser rather than trying to prove your ex-partner wrong? What freedom will you enjoy when you choose to reject the expectations that others have placed on you and opt for God's plans instead? What freedom will be shared when you choose to stop fuelling the feud in your relationships with other women and let peace in?

What freedom might multiply when you choose to conquer comparison and unleash the real you? Imagine the freedom that will thrive when you choose to stop competing with other women and instead begin to champion yourself, and them, to be who God intends us each to be!

In the next chapter we're going to see how this is possible.

14

A new grace

In the previous chapter we looked at how Esau was empowered to choose when he broke free from the burden of his relationship with his brother. We considered what freedom is still ahead for us if we determine in our hearts to conquer comparison and become a Jesus-pleaser. One of the greatest breakthroughs we will discover that will enable us to conquer comparison is when we choose to worship.

In this chapter we are going to see how a woman called Hannah discovered a life-changing freedom when she opened herself completely to the Lord. Falling to her knees, desperate and in emotional turmoil, Hannah experienced a transformation in her heart before anything in her circumstances changed.

Hannah was one of two wives to a man called Elkanah from the town of Ramathai-zophim. Peninnah was the second wife. While Peninnah had provided Elkanah with several children, Hannah was barren. Again, barrenness was pain enough, but Hannah's heartache was exacerbated by the taunting and cruelty of Peninnah – year after year after year . . .

The name Hannah comes from the Hebrew name Channah, meaning 'favour, grace'.[1] As Hannah's story unfolds we're going to see how, just as she discovered a renewed favour and a new grace to set her free, so can we.

In time Hannah would bear children and her firstborn, Samuel, would be significant in the plans of the Lord. As US pastor Frank Damazio wrote,

> Samuel the prophet–judge would lead Israel out of the tur-
> bulent times of the judges into the prosperous times of the

kings. Samuel the prophet would be a king-maker, a king-anointer and a king-confronter. His mother, Hannah, would be the foundation for his long and influential ministry to Israel. Again, God, by His sovereign hand, prepared the way for greatness through a barren woman's life of pain, sorrow, rejection and humiliation.[2]

However, before this became a reality there were years of tears and pain.

Every year, as part of their religious duties, Elkanah would take Hannah, Peninnah and her children on a 16-mile trip to the tabernacle to give sacrifices to the Lord and to celebrate his favour to them all. This was an excruciating occurrence for Hannah. It was a salt-in-wound experience that she could not avoid.

It's like the annual conference you have to attend that reminds you that your life is not how you would like it to be, or yet another wedding that reminds you of your loneliness, or that family holiday that was the goal-date for your weight loss but there's been not even a single pound drop, or that reunion that reminds you your job is not what you had hoped for. It is the why-don't-I-just-stand-here-naked moment where you wish the ground would simply open up and take you, now, but it won't and instead you have to face the pain and stifle the scream that wants to escape.

As the writer of Proverbs said, 'Hope deferred makes the heart sick, but a dream fulfilled is a tree of life' (Proverbs 13.12). In time Hannah's barrenness would be ended, but that is not known at the start of the story – and as she went, yet again, on the torturous trip to the tabernacle, Hannah felt sick.

Hannah's hope was being deferred and her heart was becoming heavier. If you have been holding out for a hope to be realized you will know her heartache. As with many of us, Hannah was constantly being tempted to compare herself with another woman, which added pressure.

'Year after year it was the same – Peninnah would taunt Hannah as they went to the Tabernacle. Each time, Hannah would be reduced to tears and would not even eat' (1 Samuel 1.7). Clearly Hannah's appetite was lost in pain – and her weakened body added to her suffering.

Like us, Hannah faced opposition. At the place of apparent safety, of worship, holy ground, the enemy was taunting Hannah. It is often when we are most tired, relaxed or unguarded that we experience our vulnerable moments and the enemy will take his opportunity to strike. It is also often in our place of safety, or imminent breakthrough, that the enemy attacks.

The Bible is not short of stories about women locked into comparison traps. However, perhaps none of them manage to keep their hearts as tender in their trials as Hannah does.

Hannah might have stopped eating and celebrating but she did not avoid worship. In fact, in a really profound moment of storytelling Hannah did not depend on the worship and sacrifice her husband made but she herself 'got up and went to pray' (1 Samuel 1.9). She did not simply ask her husband or anyone else to pray for her – she did it herself. Her pain became her prayer.

Instead of avoiding the pain she was carrying, she took herself to the place of worship and poured it out to the Lord. She longed for help from the Lord so she poured out her heart in a tender, authentic, wholehearted way.

When intercession pours from the depth of our being in such a way that words, tears and groans combine, we find a new level of breakthrough.

Consider these encouragements for how worship can be authentically released:

> Rise during the night and cry out.
>   Pour out your hearts like water to the Lord.
> Lift up your hands to him in prayer.
> (Lamentations 2.19)

Or, as David wrote,

> My life is poured out like water,
>   and all my bones are out of joint.
> My heart is like wax,
>   melting within me.
> (Psalm 22.14)

Paul also said,

> The Holy Spirit helps us in our weakness. For example, we
> don't know what God wants us to pray for. But the Holy Spirit
> prays for us with groanings that cannot be expressed in words.
> And the Father who knows all hearts knows what the Spirit is
> saying, for the Spirit pleads for us believers in harmony with
> God's own will.
> (Romans 8.26–27)

The pressure to express ourselves coherently or pray the 'right' kind of
prayers can be overwhelming sometimes. The encouragement here,
though, is to realize the empowering freedom of pouring out prayer
like water flowing from a spring – sounds that don't need vocabulary.

When Hannah took herself to the Temple to worship the
Lord she poured out her prayers so incoherently that the priest sus-
pected she was drunk! Isn't that what the disciples were accused of
being after the Holy Spirit came upon them in Acts?[3]

When was the last time your worship was misunderstood as
being the result of drinking spirits rather than fullness of the Holy
Spirit? Are we so restricted by the culture we identify with that our
worship (however that is expressed) is more of a behavioural pattern
than a heartfelt response? When we worship, is our muscle-memory
triggered so that we simply conduct ourselves on auto-drive? Do
you sing the same phrase, pray in the same way or move in the same

manner? While habits can help us establish life-giving rhythms, they must not restrict us from responding to God relationally and personally.

Hannah poured out her heart to the Lord and all the deferred hopes tumbled out of her. I don't think these were the dainty trickle of tears down her face: more like a torrent of tears tumbling down her increasingly blotchy face. Some might call these 'ugly tears' – there is no way to cry them and look 'beautiful'. But perhaps in the Lord's eyes these are the most beautiful and sincere of tears. Every tear mattered.

In a psalm written by David we can see a pivotal point of moving from the overwhelming sense of oppression from enemy attack to an awareness that heartfelt worship is received and cherished by the Lord. Even though he is slandered, attacked and afraid, David remains confident in the Lord's love.

> You keep track of all my sorrows.
>> You have collected all my tears in your bottle.
>> You have recorded each one in your book.
> My enemies will retreat when I call to you for help.
>> This I know: God is on my side!
> (Psalm 56.8–9)

In the power of the word and in a place of worship we can discover new breakthroughs, when we refuse to constrain our tears but let them flow with sincerity and authenticity, not for the attention of anyone on earth but for the worship of the Lord, knowing he catches each one in his 'bottle'. When we let down our defences we can become properly defended. It isn't about ranting to a person but pouring out our hearts to the Lord.

Hannah assured Eli the priest,

'I haven't been drinking wine or anything stronger. But I am very discouraged, and I was pouring out my heart to the LORD.

Don't think I am a wicked woman! For I have been praying out
of great anguish and sorrow.'

'In that case,' Eli said, 'go in peace! May the God of Israel
grant the request you have asked of him.'

'Oh, thank you, sir!' she exclaimed. Then she went back and
began to eat again, and she was no longer sad.

(1 Samuel 1.12–18)

Hannah's worship allowed the peace and presence of the Lord to
inhabit her such that she could eat again and was no longer sad. She
was not pregnant. She had not produced a child. Her external situation had not changed, but her internal situation was changed. Her
perspective, her outlook, her hope, her countenance, her appetite,
her confidence – everything had changed.

In the summer of 2019, as part of my sabbatical from my church
responsibilities, I was able to take a prayer and fasting retreat up
in the Rocky Mountains of Colorado Springs. During my time
there I went to a prayer cave cut into the mountains. The cave was
dark, damp and filled with bugs that I didn't really want to share
the space with. But I ventured in with the expectation of a conversation with God. I had felt him say that this was a place where I
could leave behind some stuff I didn't need any more. I'm not talking about littering, but rather a spiritual deep clean! I stood in
this cave and talked to God. As I worshipped him I let go of some
pain, disappointments, embarrassments and frustrations. And
then after a while I stepped out of the cave. I sat on the rocks in the
heat of the afternoon. Nothing had changed in my circumstances
and surroundings from before I had gone into the cave to pray.
Yet everything felt different to me. Nothing had visibly changed
but everything seemed different.

Do you remember the cave where Jesus' body was buried? After
three days the stone was found to be rolled away and the graveclothes that had once wrapped around Jesus' body were folded and

left behind.[4] The graveclothes were no longer needed, so he left them behind. He no longer needed the evidence of death because he was wonderfully alive.

There, in my little bug-infested cave, I left some 'stuff' behind. It wasn't needed any more. It was merely evidence of the sin that took Jesus to the grave. Like his graveclothes, it was no longer needed. Instead, what I needed to take away from the cave was that I was loved. I could live loved. Everything that was ahead could be lived through the lens of being loved.

Hannah didn't need the pain any more – she could leave it behind as she worshipped. She was loved. That would be enough.

What don't you need to carry any more? What can you let go of?

Hannah's story continues, 'The entire family got up early the next morning and went to worship the LORD once more' (1 Samuel 1.19). Hannah no longer needed to avoid Peninnah and her children. She no longer needed to avoid looking into the eyes of her tormentor because her eyes were on the Lord. Her worship had given her a new grace and she conquered comparison by worshipping the Lord with sincerity and passion.

Before any physical fruitfulness came to Hannah's womb, a spiritual fruitfulness came to her because she moved her focus away from her own lack and encountered the Lord's abundant love. She accepted the promise in faith as she took hold of the words spoken by Eli the priest, and chose to hope that she would see them fulfilled – one day.

The inner transformation takes place in worship as promises are accepted in faith before any eyes have seen the difference. It is the heart change that can occur as we worship with regard to our body image before any weight loss is experienced. It is the relational connecting with God in worship before any human loneliness changes.

After they worshipped, 'they returned home to Ramah. When Elkanah slept with Hannah, the LORD remembered her plea, and in due time she gave birth to a son. She named him Samuel, for she said, "I asked the Lord for him"' (1 Samuel 1.19–20).

So Hannah 'in due time' gave birth to Samuel and his lifetime lined up with a significant point in Israel's history. When Hannah was struggling in the battle of her barrenness she would have felt that her child was being withheld and that she was late in producing a baby. However, the child arrived 'in due time' – not a moment too soon and, in spite of the pain in the wait, not a moment too late – for the destiny that was on this child's life!

In understanding the time-challenge of fruitfulness within leadership, Frank Damazio writes of 'the God-part, the hidden part, the sovereign will of God being worked out quietly and secretly. The timetable is in God's hands; the purpose of God is to be fulfilled in the fullness of time.'[5]

Remember, the Lord hears the heartfelt prayers that we can't even form into words; he catches every tear poured out in worship; he holds your heart when it feels as if it is turning to wax. He sees. He hears. He knows. As Damazio says, 'prayers are often effectively heard by God long before He sends the answer' such that battles can be won, barrenness broken and 'your destiny will collide with His timekeeping to produce more than you expected for a purpose that will far exceed the hope of your petitions past'.[6]

In my own personal journey through secondary infertility, breakthrough happened when I realized (actually thanks to Frank Damazio's wisdom-filled book) that the delay in my conceiving was not so much about me but more to do with the timing of my future children's lives! Their timing and destiny was of as much interest to the Lord as mine was. He was working out a bigger plan where, thankfully, things were not all Helen-centric.

We can discover a liberty from the desire for specific outcomes when we abandon ourselves into the loving hands and purpose of the Lord. Revelation of the truth of who the Father is, even before we face a specific trial, will enable us to go through any trial with confidence in him. This is the new grace we are offered, a free gift of heaven. Even as you read this, the God who loves you invites you to pour out your pain and receive new and lasting liberty in Jesus' name.

When we can trust the one who holds all of the outcomes, the one who loves us, the one who is for us – no matter what he allows to come about – then we can discover a freedom. Our focus is lifted off our lack, our pain and our challenges and fixed on his love, his grace, his glory. It is moving focus from what *is not* to what *can be*. I think this is what Hannah discovered on the steps as she poured out her worship: her God was able – but even if he didn't provide her with a child, he was worthy of her love.

Hannah's breakthrough was messy, involved lots of tears, was open to misinterpretation but was honest. She was authentic, raw and vulnerable in her openness. Becoming a mother was not the point of breakthrough for her – the breakthrough came in her becoming an authentic worshipper. Motherhood was a gift from God. But even then motherhood did not become her identity, because once he was weaned she gave her firstborn son, Samuel, to the Lord and he grew up away from her in the Temple – serving the Lord. Hannah's breakthrough and identity were found in becoming an authentic worshipper. God responded to her honesty and set her free.

There are battles that are raging around you and within you. You may be being taunted and goaded by rivals and spiritual enemies; however, now is the time to become victorious and conquer comparisons. Now is the time to experience the abandonment of your life into the hands of the one who loves you the most with a confidence and courage in him. God is on your side. As you pour out your worship, choose to focus on him, choose to trust him, don't hold back your tears but honestly and wholeheartedly lean into him. There will be a convergence of your spirit with the Holy Spirit and the details of your destiny will come together 'in due time'. As

Hannah worshipped, God set her free – and he can do the same for you too. Now is the time to lean into the Father's love and discover freedom as you wholly worship him.

15
Hold on!

As mentioned in the previous chapter, it is often just before a break-through that we are most vulnerable to having it stolen from us. The enemy, whose goal is to keep us locked in the comparison trap and in the grip of jealousy, can prevent us from believing that there are other options. Peninnah constantly reminded Hannah that she was barren. Dare she stop comparing and believe that there could be more for her?

Recently I was visiting my parents for the day. The plan was to be there early enough to accompany them to an appointment, which meant negotiating the morning rush-hour traffic. My satnav was working very hard to find the quickest route, which meant I ended up taking unfamiliar roads. All was going well until the route took me towards a level crossing just as the barrier was descending. I pulled up to wait for the train to cross on the track before my journey could continue. I waited. Eventually a train went past and I put my car in gear ready to move. But the barrier remained down. It felt like a really long wait until the second train passed. I prepared again – but no! The barrier didn't budge. I could feel the anxiety rising in my body. Cars in front of me were bailing out, turning and heading off in the opposite direction. But I was so near my destination. Just ten minutes past this level crossing I would be at my parents' home. For me to turn around would extend my journey and potentially cause me to miss accompanying my parents. My mind was racing over all possibilities. I was flicking the map helplessly to and fro, seeing where else I might get across this train line. I was getting so tense. Should I pull out? Should I turn round? With every minute that passed and every train that zoomed past I felt more invested in the wait. I felt more conflicted about pulling out of the queue with every minute and train that passed! So I made the decision – I was going to wait it out. I was not going to quit. *Eight* trains later – *eight!* – I was finally on my way again. I reassured myself that it was good that I had waited. Perseverance had paid off. I made it to my parents' house on time.

We face trials of many different kinds, and as pressure and frustrations increase, the longing simply to give up can intensify. Remember how Hagar ran away from the trials she was facing with Sarai, but God sent her back?

When it comes to the trials we face with comparison and jealousy, the Lord is not looking for us to quit. He is not wanting us to reach for the eject button and launch ourselves to an easier place, but rather he is looking to take us *through* the trial – to discover there is more freedom the other side and there are things to learn from the journey. He wants us to hold on.

US author Lisa Bevere says, 'Comparison is a refuge for the cowardly who don't dare to believe there is something more.'[1]

In this chapter we're going to be brave and discover that there really is more for us than comparison and jealousy. What other women have, or who they are, is not our goal. They are not the measure by which we value our wholeness and success. As we conquer comparison we recognize we are incomparable. There is more for us in the purposes and plans of the Lord. But to discover the freedom of the 'more' we need to press through some pain barriers to enable us to move towards maturity.

So how do we move intentionally away from cowardice towards a comparison-free future, an outlook of confident completeness? Well, James has some ideas – although I admit at first glance they don't seem like nice ones!

James wrote to our brothers, too, but we'll keep them out of it for now:

Dear . . . sisters, when troubles of any kind come your way, consider it an opportunity for great joy. For you know that when your faith is tested, your endurance has a chance to grow. So let it grow, for when your endurance is fully developed, you will be perfect and complete, needing nothing.

If you need wisdom, ask our generous God, and he will give it to you. He will not rebuke you for asking. But when you ask him, be sure that your faith is in God alone. Do not waver, for a person with divided loyalty is as unsettled as a wave of the sea that is blown and tossed by the wind. Such people should not expect to receive anything from the Lord. Their loyalty is divided between God and the world, and they are unstable in everything they do.

(James 1.2–8)

Yay – any sort of trouble is a source of joy! Hurrah, I hear you say – not! How can tests and trials be a source of joy?

If you've ever been to a gym and braved it outside of the cardio zone then you will know muscles get strengthened when they have to push (or pull) against pressure. It is in the micro-tearing of the muscle fibres that they are stimulated to strengthen. As painful as it is, the same happens with us emotionally when our emotional muscles are exercised. *The Message* captures something interesting from James' letter:

Consider it a sheer gift, friends, when tests and challenges come at you from all sides. You know that under pressure, your faith-life is forced into the open and shows its true colours. So don't try to get out of anything prematurely. Let it do its work so you become mature and well-developed, not deficient in any way.

(James 1.2–4, *The Message*)

If I go to the gym, work out for five minutes and then quit, I am, quite frankly, getting out of it prematurely. The results won't be discernible if I don't stay and work out for a more appropriate length of time! If kids always left school mid-morning and never stayed for a full day, they would be leaving prematurely and missing out on learning. If we only ever read the first half of a book and never finished it, we would be stopping prematurely.

It is possible to be old in years and still immature – susceptible to being tossed around by the waves on the 'sea of life', as James says.

I sat with some friends recently. They were devastated to be facing an all too familiar trial that they thought would never be repeated in their life together. But now they were back, facing identical and traumatic issues, and they were hurting so much. It was heartbreaking to see. They felt as if they were circling the drain and that their relationship was all but over. They were not sure they could survive this trial again. They weren't with me to be 'fixed' and there were no simple platitudes that would have been appropriate, but there was something in my spirit that wanted to shout and declare some truths! 'This is an opportunity not to circle but to spiral upwards! It might have been the same issue but you are more mature now – you've already got the experience notched up of seeing God deliver you before. That experience could give you confidence for what God could do again. You could turn this around and become even more authentic in your life and open in your communication. You could become stronger together as your muscles flexed against the trial.'

There is hope on the other side of the hurt if you will hold on and not 'try to get out of anything prematurely', as James put it!

Jesus preached an incredible sermon all about what's on the other side of our pain and trials: we call it the Sermon on the Mount.

God blesses those who are poor and realize their need for him,
     for the Kingdom of Heaven is theirs.

God blesses those who mourn,
for they will be comforted.
God blesses those who are humble,
for they will inherit the whole earth.
God blesses those who hunger and thirst for justice,
for they will be satisfied.
God blesses those who are merciful,
for they will be shown mercy.
God blesses those whose hearts are pure,
for they will see God.
God blesses those who work for peace,
for they will be called the children of God.
God blesses those who are persecuted for doing right,
for the Kingdom of Heaven is theirs.

God blesses you when people mock you and persecute you and lie about you and say all sorts of evil things against you because you are my followers. Be happy about it! Be very glad! For a great reward awaits you in heaven. And remember, the ancient prophets were persecuted in the same way.
(Matthew 5.3–12)

On the other side of our poverty and our inability to fix all of our own issues is our dependence on God and the chance to experience God as our miraculous provider. On the other side of our grief is the opportunity to know the deepest comfort, the hope of heaven and the potential of a blessed reunion. Imagine, on the other side of the test – when we had to extend mercy to *her* when we still didn't feel *she* deserved it – is our chance to be on the receiving end of God's mercy when we definitely don't deserve it!

On the other side of that disagreement and conflict, when we had the opportunity to walk in peace and speak kindness about *her* – even when she refused to speak to us, refused to listen to us, wouldn't take any personal responsibility but blamed us for everything, removed the chance of reconciliation and instead held on to her right to anger – when we extended peace to her, expressed kindness to her, demonstrated generosity towards her – on the other side of that, we are called 'God's kids', we are being a 'chip off the old block', we are being like him!

Pressing through the tests with him, not quitting early but allowing him to help you through, you will discover even more of him. You will grow in maturity and in completeness. You will be set free.

Let's consider for a moment what it might be *to get out any of these trials prematurely* and to miss the opportunity to grow, mature and be complete. When we sort out our own pain and don't allow the Lord to help us then we will limit what we experience of him.

Getting out of trials prematurely will see us blocking, numbing, avoiding or even getting stuck in the pain. Rather than admitting and dealing with the pain, we run away from it and pretend it is not there or get trapped by it.

Dr Caroline Leaf tells of a painful personal time when she came face to face with something she had failed at:

> Instead of feeling overwhelmed with guilt and falling apart at my failure, I listened and chose to see my failure as a chance to say sorry and improve my relationship with her. I reconceptualised my failure, seeing it as a chance to do a mental 'autopsy' on what I did to make sure I never do that again . . . This type of mind-set is intrinsically hopeful; you just keep on keeping on until you are successful, while setting in place a way of analysing why you failed so you can learn what not to do next time. Indeed, being intentional about learning every time you fail is essential to success. This will allow you to appreciate the journey (with all its bumps!) and the destination. In fact, every bump can become an opportunity to learn, grow our brains, and develop mental resilience![2]

In other words: we get to grow up and move towards completeness when we go through our trials *with* Jesus!

As we come to the end of this section and agree, with the help of Christ, to hold on and not give up, we are getting ready to discover what it is to be body perfect! Before we turn to our next section, though, let's pause here with the words of Paul as we remember to hold on!

I don't depend on my own strength to accomplish this; however I do have one compelling focus: I forget all of the past as I fasten my heart to the future instead. I run straight for the divine invitation of reaching the heavenly goal and gaining the victory-prize through the anointing of Jesus. So let all who are fully mature have this same passion, and if anyone is not yet gripped by these desires, God will reveal it to them. And let us all advance together to reach this victory-prize, following one path with one passion.
(Philippians 3.13–16, *The Passion Translation*)

Part 4

BODY PERFECT

16

Broken bodies

The human body is amazing – though you might not always feel that way if you stand naked in front of a mirror. What your body can do, and has the capacity to do, is incredible! You are a complex, interconnected creation, a masterpiece!

Right from conception, as a sperm cell fertilizes an egg cell, they become a marvellous multiplying miracle! As cells divide and develop within the womb, capacity and functionality increase. The human body is not fully formed from conception, it develops over time, first inside the womb and later outside it as the child grows and develops. At birth an infant does not have the capacity to do all the things an adult can do – there is so much growth and development required.

Paul compared the Church to the human body, with feet, hands, eyes, ears and even private parts! He imagined how the relationship between each part of the Church, like each part of the human body, was in some way dependent on other parts to function and thrive. Every part of the body of the Church has a role to play that is *different from* rather than *greater or less than* another body part's function.

As we conquer comparison and consider the relationships we have with other women, we will benefit from Paul's wisdom:

Yes, the body has many different parts, not just one part. If the foot says, 'I am not a part of the body because I am not a hand,' that does not make it any less a part of the body. And if the ear says, 'I am not part of the body because I am not an eye,' would that make it any less a part of the body? If the whole body were an eye, how would you hear? Or if your whole body were an ear, how would you smell anything?

But our bodies have many parts, and God has put each part just where he wants it. How strange a body would be if it had only one part! Yes, there are many parts, but only one body. The eye can never say to the hand, 'I don't need you.' The head can't say to the feet, 'I don't need you.'

In fact, some parts of the body that seem weakest and least important are actually the most necessary.
(1 Corinthians 12.14–22)

Discovering the significance of what it is for us to be members of one 'body', and all with a part to play, will increase how we value the contribution we, and others, make. We can grow in understanding both the strengths and weaknesses of all the 'body parts'.

Throughout Scripture we can discover the beauty and the challenge of interdependent relationships. The early narratives show God referring to himself as 'us',[1] which we go on to discover through scriptural revelation is because God himself lives in triune community as Father, Son and Holy Spirit. This interconnection and oneness was then modelled and reflected in the creation of man when God didn't want him to be humanly alone,[2] so he created both male and female in his own image, interconnecting them in relationship with each other and with him. People are not designed to be isolated and completely independent, any more than a foot is designed to be the only part of the body.

Relationships between women are key body-part components which will enable the body of Christ to thrive – or not. Remember how we looked at the contagion impact of Euodia and Syntyche's relationship breakdown? Their broken relationship was threatening the mission of the church.

If you are a body part, how healthy are the interconnecting relationships you have with other women who are also part of the body? Could your relationships be stronger? Fitter?

In February 2018, hundreds of women were crowded into a church centre in Burkina Faso to enjoy the final day of a three-day women's conference – Spirit-filled, prayerful, passionate African women, all hungry to experience more of the Lord and keen to learn from his word and worship in his presence.

We were in the penultimate session exploring the delight we can all have of being a child of God. I was explaining how he is the God of all gods, the Creator of the world, the King of all kings, and yet we get to call him Daddy! I reminded my Burkinabé sisters how Paul encouraged the believers in Galatia to know the Lord as their father, Abba.[3]

There was a sense of God's pleasure and presence in the room as we celebrated how we can come as a child to our Heavenly Father – not in a child-*ish* way but in a child-*like* way.

To help the two translators Dioula and Mòoré, I preached slowly and included some 'actions' to help bring the message alive. Skipping seemed the perfect way to illustrate the liberty and freedom we have as a child of God. Unfortunately, on this occasion, this minor action caused a more-than-minor outcome as it ruptured my Achilles tendon! Thanks to my earlier wardrobe choice of an African dress I was able to tuck my injured leg up out of sight and adopted a one-legged flamingo-style posture to preach the remaining sessions. I acted as if this rupture was no more than a minor inconvenience and everything could go on as normal. But it would reveal greater repercussions in time.

How are you on Greek mythology? What about your musculoskeletal knowledge? Let's start with a little bit of Greek! In Greek mythology, Thetis was concerned by a foretelling that her son, Achilles, was going to die young, so to prevent this fulfilment she was supposed to have dipped him (head first) into the River Styx to make him immortal. Other versions of the story say she dipped him in ambrosia (which is not a delicious dessert some of us might know, but rather a treatment that included further dipping – and some fire). All of this was done as she apparently held her son by the ankles, and so the tendon at the back of the foot was undipped! Greek and Roman literature describes how Achilles was said to have died from a heel wound resulting from a puncture by a poisoned arrow in the Trojan War.

It wasn't until 1840 that our language embraced the expression of the 'Achilles heel' to describe vulnerable spots of weakness. But years later, in 2018, my Achilles heel was my Achilles heel. It felt as if it had been penetrated by a poisoned arrow!

I wonder if Paul considered the function of the Achilles tendon when he likened the Church to the human body! However, I have come to the conclusion that our omniscient Father knew how the Greek, Roman and English languages were going to develop, and just perhaps this is why our heels make an appearance even in the early creation narratives, alongside the head of the serpent![4]

I hadn't been dipped in a river (or ambrosia) but my heel was struck! During my recovery I determined that if my heel had been hurt then I would do my best to 'strike the head of the enemy'. I began to look for God in new ways, and one of the perhaps non-surprising focuses I developed was regarding the body! The more time I spent in the word of God, the more I began to see how God might be showing me something for *us* as his daughters. Can the relationships we have with other women be represented by the Achilles tendon? It is time we truly discovered what it is to be body perfect! For us to conquer comparison we would be wise to strengthen our Achilles!

My ruptured Achilles tendon required an immobilizing boot to be worn for several months, and as initially the ankle couldn't bear any weight I had to use crutches to get around. My arms were serving as my legs, and so my hands were no longer available to serve their function in the way I was previously accustomed to. They were no longer available to carry any objects because they were too busy carrying me! Simple tasks became more complicated.

In addition, I had a circulation challenge. Deep-vein thrombosis (DVT) was an increased risk because of the injury, the trauma aggravated through travelling while injured and the immobilization of the leg in the boot. As a result, for six weeks I needed to get used to a temporary drug habit – self-administering daily injections of DVT prophylaxis into my tummy to avoid fatal blood clots.

In that moment when one part of my body snapped, it affected my whole body! A tucked-away part that had previously gone unnoticed, quietly working away, had managed to cause my whole body, even my blood, to cease functioning as it was created and designed to do.

What happens to the body of Christ if its Achilles ruptures suddenly? What if relationships between women are the Achilles?

Of course, my Achilles tendon did not exert its will and choose to snap, but imagine if it had! Imagine if my Achilles had acted the way Paul described the body parts in his letter, and decided that it didn't want to function as a tendon because it considered it would be much more exciting to take on a different role. Imagine if my tendon had become jealous of my knee or hurt by my hands. Imagine if my tendon thought it was so cool that it simply didn't need any help from my foot or my calf but could go it alone. Or if my tendon was so frustrated by the weakness in my calf that it thought it would function better off without it!

All parts of the human body are essential, with unique purposes, and while, of course, many people make do, adapt, cope and even thrive with disabilities, we cannot deny the increased functionality that comes with a fully working body.

What about your part in the body of Christ? Paul's letter to the Corinthians must have caused a few chuckles as people imagined a foot wanting to be a hand. However, that is what happens! Jealousy and competition within the body cause 'feet' to want to be 'hands', 'eyes' to want to be 'noses', 'backs' to want to be 'tummies'. Surely the effect on the body of Christ is just like what happened in my body – pain and dysfunction!

For the body of Christ to thrive, for the Church to be all that she can be, we have to individually and collectively fulfil the part God has for us. We are going to discover the freedom that is ours to be who God wants us to be and the freedom we can enjoy when we empower every woman to be all that she is created to be. So how can we break free from being jealous of another body part?

Consider some of the trickier relationships you have with other women. How can we discover how to set each other free from rejection by recognizing that even if we don't naturally 'click' with someone we still *need* her! Furthermore, even if it's tricky, you can't remove yourself, because she and the whole body need you.

When my husband and I were first married we lived in a very small apartment. Learning to communicate when living in a confined space is not without its challenges. On one occasion it all regretfully became too much for me; rather than work through the pain of a conversation I decided to avoid the challenge completely – and locked myself in the bathroom. It was such a childish response to a minor verbal disagreement and offered no long-term solution! The only way forward was for me to lower my defences (and my pride), come out of hiding and have the painful conversation.

I hope you have never locked yourself in a bathroom to avoid a conversation; however, you might have muted your phone or pretended not to see someone on the other side of the street. Can we deal with our Achilles' strains before they become a full-blown rupture?

There has, sadly, been more than one occasion where I've seen women remove themselves from church for various reasons (hurt, frustrations and disappointments) and as a result they have deprived the church of their unique gifting. The body has had to work out how to function without them – which of course will happen in time. But it's not without its cost.

I've been a church leader for over 20 years and I know that the body of Christ is not immune from injury or illness. Hurtful things can happen. Leaders are not immune from either hurting others or being hurt. Most injuries caused to the body are accidents that were never intended or anticipated. Recently a friend of mine said that one Sunday she invited anyone who had ever been hurt by her to come forward. This is a courageous altar call for a church leader to give! I've been in conferences where church leaders, hurt by their congregation members, were invited to go forward for healing prayer – and there were no spaces left in the aisles!

One day I was called to the deathbed of an elderly lady. She wanted to see me before she made her final journey home and I didn't hesitate to go. I didn't know this lady exceptionally well but she was one of the sweetest people. As we held hands, tears flowed, we prepared to say our farewells and I began to pray a blessing. What happened next took me by complete surprise. Out of her mouth tumbled a torrent of accusations of things she thought I had said or thought. Terrible things. I don't know how this sweet lady had come to any of these conclusions, how long she had held these perceptions – or even how she got some of those words into her vocabulary. But in a few sacred moments I was able to assure her that I had never said or thought what she had believed. It was as if the enemy was trying to rob her of her final moments of peace. As I spoke gentle truth over her and declared God's truth about her, all the pain etched across her face seemed to melt away. We prayed and blessed one another. Just a few days later this lady woke up in heaven.

Can you see the insidious strategies of our enemy? She could have died and I would never have known about the injury she was carrying that caused a hidden rupture in our relationship. But she knew. She was limping and hurting through her last earthly days. Thank God for the gift of grace to set things right in her heart.

I am so grateful I had those moments. Of course, the conversation might have been more personally painful if I'd said, or thought, what she accused me of and had to deal with my own sin. However, it was painful enough for her and I was privileged to bc able to help her heal, while she still could.

You are part of a body. Just one part. But the part you are really needs the other parts – and they need you. Are there some ruptures that could benefit from your attention?

17

Flawsome!

Our ultimate freedom from jealousy is demonstrated when we are so liberated that we choose to champion other women rather than compete with them. But before we can become women who champion other women, we have to accept who we are ourselves! This will mean discovering which 'body part' you are and embrace being fully you.

Jesus taught his disciples that, of the original Ten Commandments given to the Israelites, there were two essential principles to live by.

> 'You must love the LORD your God with all your heart, all your soul, and all your mind.' This is the first and greatest commandment. A second is equally important: 'Love your neighbour as yourself.' The entire law and all the demands of the prophets are based on these two commandments.
> (Matthew 22.37–40)

When our focus is directed towards the Lord in every way – emotionally, spiritually, physically, mentally – then we will possess a healthy ability to express our love for ourselves and for all other people. When we love ourselves, and each other, through the lens of loving the Lord, we all thrive.

The challenge to love our neighbour is only realized when we learn to love ourselves well. The challenge to love ourselves well is only realized when we discover the wonder of knowing, really knowing, that we are loved unconditionally by God.

The one who created the universe and fixed stars in their places is the same one who created mountains, rivers, plants, animals and of course humans, who have so many things in common yet are wildly unique. It is he who knitted you together in your mother's womb, knows you intimately and *still* loves you completely. The one who knows your thoughts before they are words and sees your emotions before they show on your face. He is the one who gave up heaven to come to earth to enable you to be adopted into his eternal family. He is the one who wants you to live in his presence and for his Spirit to live within you. He is the one who longs for your first love and will enable your love for yourself and for your neighbour to flow in response.

It is Jesus' intention for us to focus on the things of God first and trust him before attending to our other concerns when he says, 'So above all, constantly chase after the realm of God's kingdom and the righteousness that proceeds from him. Then all these less important things will be given to you abundantly' (Matthew 6.33, *The Passion Translation*).

When you love the Lord with your whole, authentic, unfiltered self, you are choosing to trust and honour the one who loves you the most, the one who gave his whole, authentic, unfiltered self for you.

Within traditional Anglican wedding vows these words are often spoken between the bride and groom: 'With my body I honour you, all that I am I give to you, and all that I have I share with you, within the love of God, Father, Son and Holy Spirit.'[1] Marriage has the potential to be seen as a reflection of the closest intimacy any two people can experience – so imagine this as a commitment first and foremost between a person and the Lord. Whether you are married or not, what would it look like to honour him with your *whole self* and share *everything* with him?

As Paul wrote to the Corinthians:

Don't you realize that your body is the temple of the Holy Spirit, who lives in you and was given to you by God? You do

not belong to yourself, for God bought you with a high price. So you must honour God with your body.
(1 Corinthians 6.19–20)

Paul is encouraging the Corinthians to take great care with their body – because it doesn't actually belong to them! They've been bought with a price. Would you take greater care of yourself if you realized you were not just your own but belonged to a God who loves you more than you love yourself?

In *The Girl De-Construction Project*, Rachel Gardner sums this up beautifully:

It's not that I don't care about my body any more; in fact, I value my body *more*. If my body is the place where I experience the presence of God, I don't want to hurt the place he has made his home. If my body is the place I reach out to the world with God's love, I don't want to contradict the one I'm living for. I don't want to damage it. Not because I think I'm all that great, but because he is! Whether that's a tattoo, outfit, decision about sexual behaviour or eating plan, my body needs to tell the truth about God.[2]

Everything about who you are has the potential to be given to God in an act of worship, adoration and dedication. Everything about who you are has the potential to be something that brings him glory and shows his power. Everything about who you are has the potential to become part of God's great plan.

Learning to love God wholly and authentically will enable us to love ourselves as he intends. Our beautiful bits, our secret bits, our flawed bits – all have the potential to bring God glory.

Have you ever done any pottery? Recently I did a day's pottery class. It was hilarious, messy and much harder than it looks! We were taught the basics of how to throw, centre and then mould a pot. It was so much fun, but none of the pots I created could ever be called a masterpiece! I frequently needed rescuing by the tutor, who put her hands around the rebelling clay and with care and confidence rescued it from disaster. Pots in the hands of an expert are going to turn out well!

A prophetic artist called Lynne Pugh introduced me recently to a new word. She referred to how we can embrace being 'flawsome' – the mixture of being flawed and yet awesome. It is not being awesome *in spite of* our flaws but rather being awesome *because of* the flaws! Lynne was talking about the Japanese art of kintsugi, where broken ceramic pots have their cracks repaired with a gold or silver glue, creating beautiful renewed vessels. The cracks reveal a deeper beauty and the pot is more wonderful as a result.

If this is true for the cracks that reveal gold, how much more must it be true for our cracks that reveal God? It is time for our flaws to show their potential by revealing the Lord through them.

> We are like common clay jars that carry this glorious treasure within, so that the extraordinary overflow of power will be seen as God's, not ours. Though we experience every kind of pressure, we're not crushed. At times we don't know what to do, but quitting is not an option. We are persecuted by others, but God has not forsaken us. We may be knocked down, but not out. We continually share in the death of Jesus in our own bodies so that the resurrection life of Jesus will be revealed through our humanity.
> (2 Corinthians 4.7–10, *The Passion Translation*)

Just as our strengths can reveal Christ's grace and giftings on our lives, how much more can we reveal through the cracks and knocks?

When looking honestly at our strengths and weaknesses through the lens of God's love for us, we can discover the power of being ourselves and displaying his glory. Are you ready to be wholly you and bring all of your strengths and weaknesses, with no pretending?

Now, we would be wise to remember the order of our priorities so we don't simply blend into the cultural norms around us. Our culture encourages us to have 'me time', to put our own happiness and love ourselves first. But remember – Christ's counter-cultural distinctive way is to have *'him time'* first, to put *his* glory first and to love *him* first. It's not about us being promoted through our career first – but him. It's not us being fulfilled in our relationships first – but him. It's not our dreams becoming a reality in our life first – but his.

The beautiful revelation and freedom that we will discover (something our enemy hopes we never find out) is that when we love him first we will discover our promotions, fulfilments and dreams being realized through him. When we love him first we can love others and ourselves too.

This is beautifully demonstrated in *The Message* paraphrase of Paul's letter to the Romans. All the gifting that he identifies for different members of the body of Christ, the Church, flows from who God is. It is in loving God first, gratefully aware of his presence, that the gifts people receive can be recognized. Paul says,

I'm speaking to you out of deep gratitude for all that God has given me, and especially as I have responsibilities in relation to you. Living then, as every one of you does, in pure grace, it's important that you not misinterpret yourselves as people who are bringing this goodness to God. No, God brings it all to you. The only accurate way to understand ourselves is by what God is and by what he does for us, not by what we are and what we do for him.

In this way we are like the various parts of a human body. Each part gets its meaning from the body as a whole, not the other way around. The body we're talking about is Christ's body of chosen people. Each of us finds our meaning and function as a part of his body. But as a chopped-off finger or cut-off toe we wouldn't amount to much, would we? So since we find ourselves fashioned into all these excellently formed and marvellously functioning parts in Christ's body, let's just go ahead and be what we were made to be, without enviously or pridefully comparing ourselves with each other, or trying to be something we aren't. If you preach, just preach God's Message, nothing else; if you help, just help, don't take over; if you teach, stick to your teaching; if you give encouraging guidance, be careful that you don't get bossy; if you're put in charge, don't manipulate; if you're called to give aid to people in distress, keep your eyes open and be quick to respond; if you work with the disadvantaged, don't let yourself get irritated with them or depressed by them. Keep a smile on your face.

(Romans 12.3–8, *The Message*)

I know that, for some, there is a struggle to accept that you are good at anything. For some it can feel too difficult, more like boasting, to identify strengths. I want to encourage you to lift your eyes to our loving Heavenly Father and know that identifying and celebrating strengths can celebrate the generosity of the giver – him! As God's word says, we are each given a special grace-gift, an ability, a passion, a skill, an interest to contribute.

For instance, I have discovered I have the ability to be a gap-filler. I am seasoned enough in the ministry that I'm involved in to be able to serve effectively in many spheres – simply because, out of necessity, I've learned a lot along the way and have a commitment to see the vision fulfilled, no matter what! However, this strength could become a weakness if my involvement prohibited someone else from serving and thriving in what would be their area of strength.

When we embrace and use the gifts we've been given, we position ourselves in such a way that others have the opportunity and space to thrive in their gifts too. This is confirming again that we value and love their contribution, having loved and accepted ourselves – because we love God first.

So are you connected to the body of Christ or have you become separated? I don't mean do you know other Christians – but are you actively engaged in a local church context as a healthy member of the body of Christ? Perhaps this is the next step for you. The body needs your flawsome self to be actively bringing your best – even if that 'best' feels weak! The Lord wants to be your first love and for you to see yourself, and all others (even *her*), through the lens of his love. Will you let him help you?

18

Becoming you!

It's important to keep in mind that Jesus came to earth on a rescue-restoration mission: 'For this is how God loved the world: He gave his one and only Son, so that everyone who believes in him will not perish but have eternal life' (John 3.16). Jesus told his critics that 'Healthy people don't need a doctor – sick people do. I have come to call not those who think they are righteous, but those who know they are sinners and need to repent' (Luke 5.31–32).

It makes sense, therefore, that if those in the Christian Church are part of God's body then all of us are part of this same purpose – to express his love, through our words and actions. We are connected together to be his body – to be his arms and legs and go to all the places of the world, reaching all the people of the world. We are Jesus' body on earth at this time – and we need to work together to be the best body we can be for him.

As we've already discovered, our muscles grow stronger when they are exercised – and we grow spiritually stronger through the pressures and trials that we face. Gifts also develop and improve with use.

Have you ever heard a virtuoso musician and wished you could play like that too? A musician might have an incredible gift but will not become the best without a lot of practice. It is the discipline of practice, followed by more practice and then some more practice, that will allow the gift of musicianship to grow. So too with any gift!

The gifts we've looked at that Paul referred to in Romans were all gifts that need to be nurtured. Let's remind ourselves what he said:

In his grace, God has given us different gifts for doing certain things well. So if God has given you the ability to prophesy, speak out with as much faith as God has given you. If your gift is serving others, serve them well. If you are a teacher, teach well. If your gift is to encourage others, be encouraging. If it is giving, give generously. If God has given you leadership ability, take the responsibility seriously. And if you have a gift for showing kindness to others, do it gladly.
(Romans 12.6–8)

If you are a prophet your gifting will grow in effectiveness as you prayerfully learn to recognize the Father's voice and speak out what you hear. You can observe the message's accuracy and how it builds up and encourages others (or not!). If you are gifted in serving, you will become more helpful rather than a nuisance or in the way! Teachers will get better by refining their gift in life's classrooms and by teaching others. Encouragers will learn by speaking with people who become built up in their courage. If you say something to someone that discourages them, then be encouraged to keep practising! Generosity grows as more is given away. Leadership needs to be put it into practice, starting with self-leadership before expanding to lead someone else and then a small team, and in the refining, reviewing and retrying, leadership gifting might expand to organizations or even nations. Of course, there are many more gifts than are identified by Paul in this letter, and the list is not exhaustive. But every gift needs to be received from the Lord and used for his glory.

Gifts only become a reality when they are unlocked, released and grown, just as the character and personality of a baby are yet to be fully experienced as they develop over the years.

Paul said to Timothy,

This is why I remind you to fan into flame the spiritual gift God gave you when I laid my hands on you. For God has not

given us a spirit of fear and timidity, but of power, love, and
self-discipline.
(2 Timothy 1.6–7)

Fanning our gifts into flame rather than being afraid of them will
enable our gifts to grow and be used. This in turn brings the Father
great pleasure and glory.

None of us would ever want to give someone a gift that is never
used, that sits on a shelf ignored and unvalued. The pleasure comes
in giving a gift that is used and appreciated.

Let's put a smile on our Heavenly Father's face by using the gifts
that he has given us, in the way he intends them to be used.

Meeting at a midway point between our two distant homes, my
friend Amy and I chatted over copious quantities of tea. We turned
our conversation towards discussing what our gifts really are. My
friend is one of the most pastorally motivated people I know. She
simply loves all people and has a special grace for those others
might find challenging. She likes nothing better than meeting up
with others, one-to-one, for a cuppa and a chat, to love them and
encourage them – to pastor them. But my friend is also a leader and
has felt completely inadequate within various leadership spheres
because some have encouraged her to consider how she can take
every opportunity to 'go big'. She has been challenged not simply to
have one-to-one meetings because the strategic return on her time
investment would be so small; instead, she should be reaching 50!
She was feeling burdened and squeezed into a shape that simply
wasn't her. As we chatted she began to see how pretending to be
someone she isn't would be denying God's perfect plan. Being who
she is created to be and serving in the context of her passions, on
the other hand, would lead to God working through her. If she had
one-to-ones with just five people, and if each of them in turn
had the capacity to encourage five others, then she would be able
to encourage significantly more than just her five! Through them

she is in effect encouraging 30 people! Remember how the prophet Zechariah said, 'Do not despise these small beginnings, for the LORD rejoices to see the work begin' (Zechariah 4.10). In the Lord's hands, Amy can be free to be herself – to develop her gifting and passions – and not try to be someone else. In the Lord's hands one-to-one conversations can lead to many people being encouraged.

I've had a few friends who have aspired to have the gift of hospitality. Some have had beautiful homes which could be a great place of blessing for others, and others have been amazing at cooking. Much like Martha, they might open their door and welcome people in. But much like Martha this can come with a huge cost. The gift of hospitality is not given to a beautiful home but to a person! Some Marthas would like to walk through with a sanitizing spray whenever people arrive at their house, with outer clothes being replaced by sanitized scrubs and no outdoor shoes within a millimetre of the start of the carpeted floors. Drinks can be a hospitality nightmare for some people unless a coaster is at hand to reduce the potential for water marks. And if there are ever spills – oh, the horror! In scenarios like this the stress can be immense, for the host and definitely for her guests.

However, imagine if this Martha discovered she was *actually* really gifted in the ministries of intercession and encouragement, having the ability to persist for an issue in the place of prayer and not letting go until feeling released to do so. Or with the gift of encouragement to speak words that would build someone up, heal wounds, inspire endurance and – true to form – give courage. If she grew in her actual gifting, practised that and allowed her words to flow in prayer and encouragement, it would be amazing. Now when she offered hospitality it would not be because she wanted to impress people with her hosting skills, but rather because she was seeking to encourage them. Who wouldn't want to be a guest in this woman's home then?

Sometimes the limitations we feel on expressing our gifts do not come from ourselves but from others. I have a friend who is a gifted young leader. However, where she serves in ministry senior leadership is withheld from women – because they are women. This is a clear challenge. However, it's important to understand that gifts are what God gives and titles are what humans give. Gifts and titles are not mutually dependent as it is possible to have a great title with no gift, just as it is possible to function with mature gifts and no title. In spite of the denominational challenge, my friend is able to serve wholeheartedly and is growing in her gift of leadership even without title and official recognition.

A prophet might hold a cup of coffee rather than a microphone when speaking to the small group gathered in the coffee shop, just as a teacher never setting an adult foot in a classroom can speak life-giving wisdom to the stranger on a bus.

When God gives gifts he encourages us that the gift will make room for itself – in time doors will open.[1]

Dr Caroline Leaf writes,

You make a lousy someone else, but a perfect you, because you think in a completely unique and wonderful way. It is up to you, therefore, to design your own blueprint for success. When you find yourself comparing yourself to others stop, write down your thoughts, examine them, and think about what you are passionate about and what you have done in your own life. Think about who you are and where you want to be in life.[2]

Growing in our awareness as to what *we* are thinking enables us to take our thoughts captive and see what is in line with Christ's love. It enables us to become present in our moments and aware of how we are feeling towards other people. Being trapped in comparisons with other women will leave us living out our life as a replica when the Lord wants us to be an original. We cannot become all we are created and intended to be if we are too busy trying to be like someone else.

Teacher and motivational speaker Beth Moore said,

Reject rivalry. It rots the fruit. There's nothing one-dimensional about walking in divine gifting. God assigned gifts to each of us in full view of all coinciding components that would shape us into who we are. Genetics, gender, upbringing, ethnicity, life experiences, personality type, natural talents, skill set, relational experiences, education, intellect, emotional intelligence, health history, failures, successes, hurts, affinities, quirks, you name it. Nobody's your identical mix.[3]

In her autobiography, Michelle Obama recognized the pressure she was under to fit into a First Lady box while being expected to be unique!

I understood that I was being watched with a certain kind of anticipation, especially by women, maybe especially by professional working women, who wondered whether I'd bury my education and management experience to fold myself into some prescribed First Lady pigeonhole, a place lined with tea leaves and pink linen . . . I was supposed to stand out without overshadowing others, to blend in but not fade away.[4]

We might not become the First Lady of the United States of America, but we can become distinctly us in a way that encourages other women to become distinctly themselves. It isn't about overshadowing anyone, but being free to become ourselves so that others are free to become themselves.

There is so much expectation to blend in and connect with those around us that we can lose our distinctiveness. Remember, as we discovered in Chapter 9, what Jesus taught about the danger of salt losing its saltiness, saying:

> You are the salt of the earth. But what good is salt if it has lost its flavour? Can you make it salty again? It will be thrown out and trampled underfoot as worthless.
>
> You are the light of the world – like a city on a hilltop that cannot be hidden. No one lights a lamp and then puts it under a basket. Instead, a lamp is placed on a stand, where it gives light to everyone in the house. In the same way, let your good deeds shine out for all to see, so that everyone will praise your heavenly Father.
>
> (Matthew 5.13–16)

He was talking to his disciples about being distinct as a Christ-follower such that they would be beneficial to the world around them. Salt brings out the flavour, preserves, cleanses and even enhances fertilizer to increase the fruitfulness of plants. Jesus wants us to enhance the world's flavours, preserve that which is great, cleanse that which needs it and encourage fruitfulness around us. He doesn't want us to blend in and disappear into blandness. Jesus invites you to be the light in the darkness – bright, distinct and visible, not hidden away – such that *everyone will praise the Lord*. Using your gifting, according to the grace you've been given, is definitely one way for you to 'shine'.

Now here lies a challenge. The motivation to be completely ourselves can lead us to want to self-satisfy, become self-fulfilled and bring attention to ourselves. Being satisfied and fulfilled are not wrong unless they become our goals. Jesus taught that when we are truly who God has made us to be, distinct and light in the dark place, then it will not so much draw attention to ourselves but rather draw attention to God – our creator.

In the celebrity culture that we live in we are encouraged to be the best version of ourselves, often with the aim of drawing attention to how great we are. Jesus taught that in him we can be a new version of ourselves, authentic, whole and unique, and in turn draw attention to our Heavenly Father, seeing his purposes fulfilled. Freedom is ours when we don't crave to be liked because we're confident we're loved. When our social media platforms don't serve to validate us but rather express us and encourage others.

It is only when we become fully his that we can truly become ourselves. As we give ourselves to him and accept how he has given himself to us we can become all that he has created and intended us to be. When we become who we are divinely designed to be, we will not be threatened or jealous of anyone else – because our eyes will be on him and not turning green towards other people!

19

Daddy's girl

I have two dads. They are both amazing yet very different. My biological dad brought up me and my sister, and has always been meticulously careful to be completely fair. If he gives a gift to one of us he will work out the exact costings to give the other one a gift of equal value. His generosity is not means-tested to the recipient's perceived or actual needs.

My second dad is not so predictable. Perhaps it's because he's got more children. I know he loves me but he doesn't treat all his kids the same. He tells me that he is always the same, never-changing, and while I'm convinced his character doesn't change, his behaviour does! Several of us ask what seems to be the same question but we each get very different answers! Some of us can turn up with seemingly the same needs, and yet we are rarely (if ever) met with the same response. Certainly, some of us have been heard to moan repeatedly that we're being treated unfairly. We might not say it to his face (although sometimes we will) but we will say it among the rest of the family, or outside the family: he doesn't seem to treat us all the same.

I think my biological dad enjoys being predictable. For so many years he has been my human rock, reliable and consistent – not in a boring manner but in a genuine, authentic, solid way. My second dad is not the same – his love is consistent and reliable while he seems to be unpredictable, and I'm convinced he chuckles when I'm caught off guard on occasions. Not in a mean way – in a sort of pleasure-from-surprising-me kind of way. I'm not saying he is not genuine, authentic, solid or reliable, just that he can announce something that seems to be a game-changer – often!

One of the hallmarks to my biological dad's early parenting success was in bringing up me and my sister to be independent adults. We are still relationally interconnected with him but able to stand on our own two feet, bringing up our own families and being 'grown up'. My second dad is more intent on wanting me, and his other kids, to be – well, more childlike. He challenges me to grow up, to be less childish when I'm being immature (he's not a fan of my tantrums) but at the same time he tells me that he will always be my daddy!

Jesus had two dads, and although we don't hear a huge amount about his earthly dad, Joseph, we do hear a lot about his Heavenly Father. As Jesus taught and showed his disciples how to get to know his Heavenly Father, he seemed to expect them to learn that he, like my second dad, might appear somewhat unpredictable in his responses to them.

In a parable that Jesus taught, he addressed the matter of apparent fairness by telling a story of a landowner who was hiring staff for a day's work. This man went out early to hire workers for his vineyard and agreed to pay them the normal daily wage. A few hours later, while the first workers were already hard at work, the landowner went back into town and hired more workers on the basis that at the end of the day he would pay them whatever was right. Three times during the day the landowner went back into town and hired more workers. Even just an hour before everyone was clocking off for the day, he hired some more workers. At the end of the day all the workers gathered together to receive their pay. The ones who had only worked for an hour were paid first and received a full day's salary. The first recruits assumed they would receive a healthy bonus. Yet when their turn came they received an identical amount – the previously agreed amount for the day. This didn't seem fair, given they had worked a full day and the others had just sneaked in for an hour. So they complained to the landowner because he was treating them unfairly. His response?

The landowner replied, 'Friends, I'm not being unfair – I'm doing exactly what I said. Didn't you agree to work for the standard wage? If I want to give those who only worked for an hour equal pay, what does that matter to you? Don't I have the right to do what I want with what is mine? Why should my generosity make you jealous of them?'
(Matthew 20.13–15, *The Passion Translation*)

Why should the generosity and kindness of the landowner towards some people make the others jealous of *them*? But yet 'That's not fair!' tumbles so easily from our lips.

A while later, resurrected Jesus was breakfasting on fish with his disciples and got into a conversation with Peter, which concluded with a prediction of how Peter's life would end. Peter started comparing himself to fellow disciple John and wanted to know what John's future might be, only to be met by the response from Jesus that 'If I decide to let him live until I return, what concern is that of yours? You must still keep on following me!' (John 21.22, *The Passion Translation*).

It is apparent that Jesus' first disciples were challenged in comparing not only what they received during their earthly life by means of day-to-day reward for effort, but also how their earthly life was going to end! The first disciples clearly wanted a humanly perceived fairness from the Lord, with each of them being treated equally, and when that didn't happen there was jealousy between them.

Let's be honest with ourselves – do we fall into the same temptation of observing the blessing someone else enjoys and becoming jealous of what the Father is doing in that person's life, because we feel he should be giving us the same too? Have you ever felt God has treated you unfairly and become jealous of the recipients of his generosity and kindness? In living and even in dying, are there jealous responses projected towards those recipients of the Lord's generosity?

It is with shame that I confess I have looked at the lives of other people and been jealous of the favour they've received! I have fallen into the trap of comparison and felt hard done by, as if I've been short-changed. As if they've got something that I should have been given. As if I should have received more. As if I deserved what they were enjoying. Most often this has been through the lens of social media.

With every jealous twitch in my spirit or swipe with my finger, I miss the point of grace! I have never deserved any of the blessings that I've received. I've been a recipient of God's Riches At Christ's Expense (GRACE) time after time, day after day, second after second! I have been the recipient of mercy, in that I've not received what I have deserved in consequence for my sin, but at the same time the recipient of what I haven't deserved in the grace-gift of eternal life. And the same is true for you!

The early disciples had a knowledge of Father God but were getting to know him through the eyes, and life, of Jesus. To trust that the Father was not being unfair when he treated them differently required them to get to know him more. We can get to know the Father the same way – through Jesus.

As I clung to the side of the mountain, the descent looked ominous. Others had made the abseil look easy but my courage had vanished and abandoned me to my fear. The instructor, clearly not wanting to be stuck with me there for ever, tried to encourage me that the harness was more than capable of holding me securely and I just needed to lean out and go. 'Trust me,' he said, 'you can do this.' My nervous response wasn't meant to be rude but came out as 'I can't trust you – I don't know you!' So many people acknowledge that trust is not to be assumed but is to be earned. Arguably, the instructor's training should have *earned* him my trust. However, as I hung in my harness on the mountainside it seemed that trust was more relational than academic.

The vineyard workers had to learn this about their boss, just as the disciples – and all of us, too – have the chance to learn this about our heavenly dad. Will we choose to get to know him more and trust him more – confident that he has our best interests in his heart and mind? Even if things don't seem 'fair', will we trust him?

The writer of Proverbs says, 'Trust GOD from the bottom of your heart; don't try to figure out everything on your own. Listen for GOD's voice in everything you do, everywhere you go; he's the one who will keep you on track' (Proverbs 3.5–6, *The Message*).

I have two dads. They are both amazing, yet very different. My biological dad brought me up lovingly and faithfully to stand on my own two feet and become an independent grown-up. My second dad is my heavenly dad, who is bringing me up to depend on him, not stand on my own feet, but who invites me to enjoy the journey, just like a child putting her feet on top of her daddy's to dance – a limitless adventure getting to know him.

However many dads you might be able to count in your story so far – and whatever the experience of the human dads in your life that you've experienced – you can be the daughter of our heavenly dad. You too can be Daddy's girl. So let me ask you some questions. *So what* if he chooses to give somebody else something you like? *So what* if he chooses to give you something that someone else would like? *So what* if he chooses to be generous in an unpredictable way? He has given you grace. He has given you mercy. We can exchange our jealousy and comparisons for limitless joy, peace, gratitude and more!

Are you willing to stand on Daddy's feet and enjoy the next dance? On his toes we're going to discover that one of our greatest freedoms is received when we look to celebrate and champion other women. We're going to dance our way to conquer comparison!

Part 5

CREATED TO CHAMPION

20

She-witnesses

As we live jealousy-free, comparison-free and dancing on our daddy's toes, we will discover something very powerful – we can help to set other women free too!

Remember Paul's letter to the Romans when he encouraged his readers to be confident that

> Just as our bodies have many parts and each part has a special function, so it is with Christ's body. We are many parts of one body, and we all belong to each other. In his grace, God has given us different gifts for doing certain things well. So if God has given you the ability to prophesy, speak out with as much faith as God has given you. If your gift is serving others, serve them well. If you are a teacher, teach well. If your gift is to encourage others, be encouraging. If it is giving, give generously. If God has given you leadership ability, take the responsibility seriously. And if you have a gift for showing kindness to others, do it gladly.
> (Romans 12.4–8)

Paul wanted the believers to be fully *who* they were called and created to be. He then continued his letter to the Christ-followers in Rome with a further challenge, saying, 'Don't just pretend to love others. Really love them. Hate what is wrong. Hold tightly to what is good. Love each other with genuine affection, and take delight in honouring each other' (Romans 12.9–10).

Some people, of course, are easy to love – but many are not. So this is a great challenge to us today, just as much as to its first audience. How do we really love people? How do we know when we are simply pretending? We will only be able to end jealousy towards other women, to such a degree that we will embrace our real freedom and become women who champion other women, when we stop play-acting and start being *real* in our love.

In a slow blink we can be skilled scanners! We can scan a person from head to toe while pretending to blink and silently make an immediate assessment. The hair, the make-up (or lack of it), the clothes (or lack of them) – shape, colour, cut – it's all observed in a nanosecond. We pretend we don't do it, but many of us are highly gifted in making an immediate assessment about another woman simply by how she appears!

Have you ever had the scroll-and-roll experience: as you scroll through social media sites, your eyes fall on an image and their reflex response is to roll? The more you look at certain images the more your eyes roll and your tongue tuts. As you scroll through the social media feeds and roll your eyes – at what she's wearing this time, what she's doing this time, what she has said this time – with each eye roll there is another nanosecond of judgement accruing in your heart against her.

Recently I passed a lady on the stairs of a conference centre. She paused to greet me. I met her in passing and we shared the briefest of 'hellos' before this lady commented on an Instagram photo I'd been tagged in. It was a family celebration where we were gathered around the table. I'm never one to really appreciate food photography and, definitely, if I'm the cook (as I was on this particular occasion) I'm more interested in my guests eating the food while it's hot rather than the food going cold so the perfect photo can be shot. Anyway, this lady on the stairs advised me that she liked the photo and had zoomed in to see what was on my plate! She wanted to know what I was actually eating. She scrolled-and-rolled, in a nanosecond of judgement on what I was eating, and then felt the need to share it with me in person as well!

You may have noticed that on occasions some people's fingers and thumbs seem braver than their tongues. Status updates often get published that I'm confident would not be said in a face-to-face encounter.

There is one woman who lived many years ago who, if she had lived in the social media age, would probably have succumbed to many a scroll-and-roll from her community as well as many harsh thumb wars on some online comments. This lady has been called some harsh names because she had a history of partners. She was in a partnership with a man at the time she met Jesus, but before that had lived through five marriages. From John's account we are not told why her marriages have failed but cultural understanding might suggest that she has been repeatedly widowed and may have even been subject to the ancient traditions and 'passed on' to the dead husband's brother or the nearest relative who could serve as her 'redeemer'. The patriarchal set-up gave ludicrous freedom to men to be able to discard a woman through divorce for the most trivial of reasons, so perhaps this had happened.

Either way, heartache and hardship had travelled with this tenacious survivor. Her relationship with the women of the town was not positive. This is not explicitly said by John, but the custom of the time was for the women to go to the well for water together in the cooler, earlier mornings. This Samaritan woman came alone – in the heat of the day.

Jesus had been travelling in the area and was returning with his disciples from Judea to Galilee. He decided to take a slight detour and go through Samaria on the way. Stopping at Jacob's well, he sent his disciples into the village to get supplies. He didn't have to wait long before this lady arrived. Asking her for a drink of water, Jesus went against all cultural expectations by talking with her. Then he told her, 'If you only knew the gift God has for you and who you are speaking to, you would ask me, and I would give you living water' (John 4.10).

A beautiful conversation unfolded, which disarmed any defences this lady might have built up and instead enabled her to experience first hand the love of Christ. What then happened was incredible. The woman left her jug at the well and ran back to the village. She went excitedly around her village, inviting anyone who would listen to come and meet Jesus – most likely, even the very women who didn't want to be seen at the well with her. She invited them all to meet this man who might 'possibly be the Messiah' (John 4.29). She was not one to keep something so good to herself.

This lady is credited with being the first female evangelist of her day. She became a witness to what she had experienced of Jesus, and as a result many of her village came to meet with Jesus and be saved by him. Her willingness to be a witness brought about community transformation.

Here is a key for us in the challenge of being free enough to set her free. Transformation will come into all our relationships, with our ability to really love people (not pretend), when we live as a witness and not as a judge. It is time to end the scroll-and-eye-roll.

Consider in a law court the two distinct roles of witness and judge. A witness is a person who sees an event, an incident or an action, and then has the opportunity to describe it. This is someone who reads the room, observes and reflects what is seen. A judge is someone who is given authority for a time frame and empowered to form an opinion or conclusion about a person, event or action.

For many years my dad served as Chair of the Magistrates in our local court. He would listen to both prosecution and defence as cases were presented and witness accounts were given, using the power and authority bestowed upon him and his fellow magistrates to bring a judgement. He was required to bring the proceedings to a conclusion by making a decision. The witnesses were never required to do that. They just had to give an honest reflection on what they had seen and heard. My dad was rarely able to divulge the details of the court's proceedings to his inquisitive family but we were familiar with seeing the pressure of responsibility weigh heavily on him. The position of serving in judgement was a privilege for him, but it carried a huge emotional burden.

Many times Jesus encouraged his disciples to live ready to give an account of what they had seen. Whether this was in a court of law as they faced trial for their faith or in the day-to-day conversations of making disciples, they were encouraged to tell those around them what they had seen Jesus do. Just before Jesus returned to be with his Father in heaven, he instructed his disciples to wait for the Holy Spirit and then to expect their partnership with the Spirit to enable them to be even greater witnesses.

> Then he said, 'When I was with you before, I told you that everything written about me in the law of Moses and the prophets and in the Psalms must be fulfilled.' Then he opened their minds to understand the Scriptures. And he said, 'Yes, it was written long ago that the Messiah would suffer and die and rise from the dead on the third day. It was also written that this message would be proclaimed in the authority of his name to all the nations, beginning in Jerusalem: "There is forgiveness of sins for all who repent." You are witnesses of all these things.
>
> 'And now I will send the Holy Spirit, just as my Father promised. But stay here in the city until the Holy Spirit comes and fills you with power from heaven.'
> (Luke 24.44–49)

There is a power partnership available to us when we allow the Holy Spirit to work within us to enable us to be a witness for Jesus.

I've always understood that being a witness of my relationship with Christ is important when connecting with those who don't yet have a relationship with him. But what if being a witness becomes a lifestyle, our relational approach with everyone – absolutely everyone?

Imagine what this could do for our relationships if we approached every relationship, every conversation and every human encounter as a witness for Jesus rather than as a judge!

As I was driving away from the gym recently I gave way to a young woman walking towards the local college so that she could cross in front of me. She was wearing headphones and came to the edge of the pavement and continued walking across the road without so much as a pause. I didn't notice any movement in the direction her head was facing – but as she walked forward in front of me she raised her left hand and gave me a thumbs-up for stopping. Just a thumbs-up, without so much as a glance in my direction. I mean, this girl must have been like a lizard with such phenomenal peripheral vision that she didn't need to look both ways before crossing the road! Or was she so confident that all traffic would stop for her that she walked regardless of whether I stopped or not? I was amused by this young woman. But I knew what the Lord had placed on my heart for women's freedom and I recognized in these moments that I could approach this girl either as a witness or as a judge. So I spent the next few minutes of my journey working out the difference. Responding as a judge, my mind saw this girl as lizard-girl. She had peripheral vision and a selfishness to keep in her music zone oblivious to the traffic or the consequences of her actions on others. Regarding this girl in the posture of a judge, I could see her as arrogant and with poor judgement because she had not even taken a momentary pause to check the road. Oh, and of course she was ignorant of road safety! Look how easy it is for me to see myself as a judge.

Then I asked the Lord to help me approach her like a witness – a witness who has seen who Jesus is and how he came to earth for everyone. As the Holy Spirit moved within me I could see that this young woman had been made with the ability to think quickly. She saw me before I saw her and then she noticed I was slowing as I approached. The Lord had given her a confidence because he longs for her to be a culture-shaper and an influencer among her peers rather than someone who is easily misled. As she was knitted within her mother's womb the Lord had a plan for her and knew what her dreams would be. He had enabled her to be willing to keep learning, not avoiding college but rather heading there. Furthermore, she accepted her responsibility to get herself there – under the effort of her own two feet. So she was contributing to reducing the carbon footprint and improving her own health by walking. This young woman was amazing, and for any thumbs-up she gave me the Lord had given her the thumbs-up long before.

It was so much more fun looking at this young girl through the lens of Jesus' love for her. It was so much more fun witnessing to what Jesus was doing in and around her than it was assuming the posture of a judge and mocking her for her behaviour, rolling my eyes when she didn't even turn her head or tutting that I was given a thumbs-up rather than a nod or a smile.

When Paul wrote in his letter to the Romans that they were to really love one another and not pretend, he followed up with the challenge always to be ready to give honour. I heard recently that we can give honour to anyone, not depending on what we deem them worthy to deserve but out of what we personally carry. The idea is that we can only give away what we have. The same principle can be applied to how we speak – at every opportunity – as a witness because we can only really appreciate what Jesus is doing if we know who Jesus is. So the closer we get to him, the more we are able to witness to what he is doing.

A lifestyle that Jesus showed us is seeing what the Father is doing and joining in!

Jesus explained, 'I tell you the truth, the Son can do nothing by himself. He does only what he sees the Father doing. Whatever

the Father does, the Son also does. For the Father loves the Son and shows him everything he is doing.'
(John 5.19–20)

When we love God first, and fully, we are able to love ourselves – which will empower us to really love other people. When we approach everyone with the honour that we've received from Christ, we can experience the power of the Holy Spirit, who will enable us to see what Jesus is doing in them. We can be a witness to Jesus, and honour towards others will pour out of us. It is as John wrote, 'We love each other because he loved us first' (1 John 4.19).

Try it today – I dare you! Every person that you see, whether in passing or in conversation, in the news or on your social media screen, is someone who can be a recipient of honour from you. So, without faking it, be a witness for who Christ is and what he is doing around every individual. What does he feel towards each one? Through the power of the Holy Spirit working in you, say what he sees about every person. What is the Father already lovingly saying about each one? Will you join in?

As you practise this you will enable your posture to move from judge to witness.

Jesus revealed his resurrected self first to women, who had gathered together to give comfort and strength to one another.

Early on Sunday morning, as the new day was dawning, Mary Magdalene and the other Mary went out to visit the tomb.

Suddenly there was a great earthquake! For an angel of the Lord came down from heaven, rolled aside the stone, and sat on it. His face shone like lightning, and his clothing was as white as snow. The guards shook with fear when they saw him, and they fell into a dead faint.

Then the angel spoke to the women. 'Don't be afraid!' he said. 'I know you are looking for Jesus, who was crucified.

He isn't here! He is risen from the dead, just as he said would happen. Come, see where his body was lying. And now, go quickly and tell his disciples that he has risen from the dead, and he is going ahead of you to Galilee. You will see him there. Remember what I have told you.'

The women ran quickly from the tomb. They were very frightened but also filled with great joy, and they rushed to give the disciples the angel's message. And as they went, Jesus met them and greeted them. And they ran to him, grasped his feet, and worshipped him. Then Jesus said to them, 'Don't be afraid! Go tell my brothers to leave for Galilee, and they will see me there.'

(Matthew 28.1–10)

These women were commissioned to become witnesses as they met with Jesus. He told them to go and give a report to the grieving disciples. The disciples, who were confused, devastated and fearful having lost Jesus, were given great courage from these women as they witnessed to the reality of Jesus' resurrection, such that the disciples would be given hope. Before even personally encountering resurrected Jesus they would again have hope and courage. Faith would arise within them activated by the witness of the women. Such is the power of partnership with the Holy Spirit when we become witnesses. The women didn't keep the good news to themselves or use their revelation as leverage to condescend or judge the disciples, but rather inspired and encouraged them.

Instead of looking at someone and allowing judgement to rise, we are invited by the Lord to be his witness. We get to say what we see him do and tell what we hear him say. What a privilege! We don't need to be a judge of anyone, including other women, but instead we can witness to them about Jesus. The move from judge to witness is the beginning of our freedom. When you see Jesus you can say what he sees, put competition and jealousy aside and begin to champion women.

21

Wearing L-plates

Let's stick with the challenge of *really* loving one another until the pretence truly fades.

As I sat behind the learner driver at the junction, wondering if she would ever find the correct gear, I had two choices of what would be *my* next move. I don't mean in a car-moving sort of way as it was clear we were not going to go anywhere fast. I mean in attitude. As I stared at the red L, I could wait, patiently, mindful that I too was once a traffic-slowing learner driver, or I could choose to be impatient and frustrated that I was being thwarted in my attempt to get on with my busy-and-oh-so-important day. And it is even harder when we don't see any L-plates and yet we are stuck behind drivers who don't seem to know what they are doing or suddenly do something unpredictable or drive in such a way that we are getting delayed! When our *right* to be where we want to be, when we want to be there, is interrupted, it can be frustrating.

The challenge 'don't just *pretend* to love others – *really* love them'[1] is easy with some people, but what about those tricky ones! Perhaps you have never experienced this kind of inconvenience on the road, but I'm pretty sure you will have experienced something like this in your relationships: when someone behaves unpredictably and throws a curve-ball your way that forces you to respond, when someone's immature response or insensitive quip reveals the lack of depth to their understanding, or perhaps when someone's behaviour is so pre-dictably irritating that your patience and grace get up and go. Perhaps relational L-plates would be helpful for us all to wear! To authentically 'own' our personal L-plates is to live transparently, not pretending to be 'all sorted' but still seeking to grow honestly and learn.

When it comes to learning about relationships Paul's letter to the Corinthians is hugely helpful (albeit challenging!). It's a passage that has been popularized at weddings but was not intended exclusively for these occasions. There is a lot for women to learn from Paul's letter to the Corinthians. However much we successfully function according to our gifts and thrive in our 'body part' for Christ, if we do this without being identified with an 'L' for love then we are not going to be relating to others well. Love is an area where we need to remain living as learners!

> If I could speak all the languages of earth and of angels, but didn't love others, I would only be a noisy gong or a clanging cymbal. If I had the gift of prophecy, and if I understood all of God's secret plans and possessed all knowledge, and if I had such faith that I could move mountains, but didn't love others, I would be nothing. If I gave everything I have to the poor and even sacrificed my body, I could boast about it; but if I didn't love others, I would have gained nothing.
>
> Love is patient and kind. Love is not jealous or boastful or proud or rude. It does not demand its own way. It is not irritable, and it keeps no record of being wronged. It does not rejoice about injustice but rejoices whenever the truth wins out. Love never gives up, never loses faith, is always hopeful, and endures through every circumstance.
>
> Prophecy and speaking in unknown languages and special knowledge will become useless. But love will last forever!
> (1 Corinthians 13.1–8)

In his book *How to Like Paul Again*, Conrad Gempf of the London School of Theology says,

> 1 Corinthians is telling us post-modern westerners that we need to love each other and think more in terms of 'out-dated'

notions of courtesy and respect than in terms of rights and freedoms. Perhaps, for different reasons, we find ourselves in a culture that behaves very similarly to the Corinthians. We want attention; we want the advantages that we believe are our rights. And if anything keeps us from these, we, like the Corinthians, look for sympathy and redress, sometimes even redress in the courts.[2]

One of the biggest partners to jealousy that damages relationships between women and prohibits us from championing one another is unforgiveness, in the form of keeping records of being wronged. This will show itself in the absence of our 'Love plates'! We've stopped learning to love in the way that Christ intends. The right to retain the pain of being wronged by another woman has crippled and ruined many female relationships. Holding on to the hurt from *her* by keeping the record of wrongs alive will rob you of the freedom to be all that you could be, and will restrict other relationships you are involved in from thriving.

You might look perfectly healthy from the outside, but being a keeper of records of being wronged will become toxic within you. Holding on to unforgiveness will hurt you more than the perpetrator of the issue. Yet extending forgiveness can be so very hard when the pain is so real. Again, the solution is in keeping our eyes on Christ.

Through the complete resurrection-work of Christ, through the cross, *our* sins are dealt with:

> He does not punish us for all our sins;
>> he does not deal harshly with us, as we deserve.
> For his unfailing love toward those who fear him
>> is as great as the height of the heavens above the earth.
> He has removed our sins as far from us
>> as the east is from the west.
> (Psalm 103.10–12)

God has decided that when it comes to *our* sins, because of Christ he will forgive us and choose not to remember them, saying, 'And I will forgive their wickedness, and I will never again remember their sins' (Hebrews 8.12).

God has determined that he will not even think about *our* sins and so they are no longer in his short-term, medium or long-term memory: 'I – yes, I alone – will blot out your sins for my own sake and will never think of them again' (Isaiah 43.25).

He is not keeping a record of wrongs against us – he is not revisiting our sins against him – he is not harbouring the hurt that we've caused him – he is not even thinking about it!

Because the Lord chooses not to remember our sins, we are invited to live in the freedom that comes when our sins are removed from us. We can move in the gift of living free from guilt and shame, free to be who we are called and created to be in the Lord.

As we saw in Chapter 5, forgiveness is not simply forgetting a wrong has occurred but rather is choosing not to remember the wrong. We can be on the receiving end of the Lord's grace and forgiveness. He will not remember our sin and so we don't need to either. Here is a tension; we don't need to remember *what* we've been forgiven but we must remember that we *have been* forgiven.

If we take our eyes off Jesus' sacrifice on our behalf we can drift into entitlement, as if we deserve grace. If we forget *how* we've been forgiven we will forget that we *needed* to be forgiven in the first place. As soon as this drift has begun, we will hold on to our rights in such a way that we will not readily extend grace to others and instead hold to the right to retain the pain others cause us.

Girls, be honest – how long is your record of wrongs against *her*, or *them*?

Lincoln Brewster wrote a song called 'Surrender', which encourages us to lay down our rights – even those rights to retain the pain – for the freedom that comes with new life in Christ. Brewster goes on to suggest that this is only possible because of 'waiting at the cross'. We must not rush away from the miraculous exchange that takes place at the cross. Rather, like the women in Jesus' time, we are wise to wait at the cross a little longer.

Remember how we looked earlier at the way Matthew captures a conversation in his Gospel between Jesus and his disciples. Peter asked, "'How many times do I have to forgive my fellow believer who keeps offending me? Seven times?" Jesus answered, "Not seven times, Peter, but seventy times seven times!"' (Matthew 18.21–22, *The Passion Translation*). Jesus went on to tell a story about a rich man forgiven a huge debt, who wouldn't extend even a tiny bit of grace towards someone who owed him a minor debt. In the context of eternal living and the number of wrongs that I've committed against the Lord, there is nothing that any person can do against me that will begin to balance the grace I've received. However much I've been wronged, there is nothing that will outweigh how much I've wronged him. And the same is true for you.

No matter how much we've been wronged it will not outweigh how much we have wronged the Lord, yet he chooses to forgive, to not think about or remember what we've done wrong. You have received limitless grace, complete forgiveness and a freedom to live guilt-free. Isn't it time to extend some of what you've received to *her*, or *them* – stop keeping a record of wrongs and set her free? Because we are good at holding on to the negative stuff it's not always easy to destroy the record of wrongs. Yet the Lord's grace is sufficient – and he will help us.

As Paul wrote, 'Love never gives up, never loses faith, is always hopeful, and endures through every circumstance' (1 Corinthians 1.7). Such is the Lord's love for you. This enduring, hopeful, faithful, persistent love will enable you to do what otherwise would be impossible, even after you've been hurt – to try again! To risk again. To befriend again. To love again. While new boundaries might be essential after something wrong has taken place, and some relationships won't be activated again, it is openness to the work of the Holy

Spirit that restrains us from building 'just-in-case' barriers between us to keep us defended.

In his book *The Anointing*, pastor and teacher R. T. Kendall describes what it is to be open to the work of the Holy Spirit in our minds but not in our hearts, and the risks that ensue in our relationships with each other.

It is possible to be theoretically open (open in theory – that is, we give intellectual assent) but closed in our hearts. Why would we be open in the head but not the heart? The chief impediment to openness to the Spirit is fear. 'For God did not give us a spirit of timidity, but a spirit of power, of love and of self-discipline' (2 Tim. 1.7). We must become vulnerable: able to be hurt. Becoming vulnerable means that we are willing to be hurt – or embarrassed. We must cease protecting ourselves with things such as defence mechanisms (setting up defences in our minds) or excuses for not being involved or worrying about our reputation with friends – even closest friends.[3]

Kendall is not talking about abusive relationships, because we do need to be protected against them. But in the majority of our relationships with women we will all thrive when any negative narrative of what has been is not allowed to define what can or will be – when we are willing to hold on to hope even when it requires taking a risk. Perhaps there is no greater risk in modern relationships than letting go of controlling our reputation. Kendall acknowledges that

The paramount stigma of today's man or woman is probably that of being misunderstood. Nothing is more painful than this. We can cope with a lot that people say against us as long as they are fully in the picture and still disagree. But what *hurts* is when they *aren't* in the picture and form judgements and perceptions that are based on limited information.[4]

The truth of the matter, though, is that we are all learning what it is to live lovingly. As much as we want to *be understood*, we would be wise to put our L-plates on and admit we are still learning what it is to *understand*.

There is relational challenge when we long to be understood for our intentions while retaining the 'right' to view others through their actions. When we receive clumsy words and ill-thought-out actions we are quick to assume the intent even when we are not fully in the picture.

Do you remember how the devil was able to slip into the skin of the serpent to persuade Eve to disobey God? Years later Jesus rebuked one of his closest disciples, Peter, for mis-speaking when he tried to redirect what the Lord was doing and so got the strong rebuff of 'Get away from me, Satan! You are a dangerous trap to me. You are seeing things merely from a human point of view, not from God's' (Matthew 16.23). If the enemy can masquerade inside the snakeskin in the Garden, surely he can masquerade even in the unaware *her*. If the enemy can speak through Peter (on whom the Church was going to be built!) then surely he can occasionally speak through the unguarded *her*!

When Jesus hung on the cross he asked his Heavenly Father to forgive the soldiers 'for they don't know what they are doing' (Luke 23.34). The soldiers did know that they were carrying out Roman rule as they executed Jesus, but they were ignorant of the underlying human and spiritual agendas being worked out.

This is not to create suspicion but rather to increase discernment and wisdom. We have a very real enemy who is hell-bent on stealing and destroying life. *She* is not your enemy – but the devil is! An enemy determined to steal heaven's souls for his own gain. An enemy set on dividing relationships between women to prevent the Lord's love from being demonstrated between us. We should not give him the privilege of pulling our strings or of tricking us to walk in his snakeskins! (That's not a fashion statement – if you want to wear snakeskin print then go ahead and rock the look, but we must all stay clear of being hijacked by the one who is against us.)

As Kendall says with regard to us all stepping into the purposes and anointing that Christ has for our future, we have to wise up to who is our actual enemy:

> When we learn to forgive one another totally and come to see our pitiful bankruptcy, we will be getting close to tomorrow's anointing. When we cease attacking one another and worry about the Philistines outside the family rather than competing with one another, we will be getting close.[5]

As this chapter concludes, can we all agree that, when it comes to love, we all have much to learn? Who can you extend grace to today?

22

Let him leap!

As we practise loving one another, aware we are each wearing L-plates and growing as a witness (not a judge), we will be growing more like Christ and relationships will continue to thrive. Love really does make a difference. As *The Message* paraphrase says, 'Most of all, love each other as if your life depended on it. Love makes up for practically anything' (1 Peter 4.8).

The more we love each other as Christ loved us, the more we live outside of the comparison trap – free. The more we live freely, the more we will want others to live freely too! Love will strengthen the motivation in us to become women who champion other women. We will celebrate, encourage and cheer on other women into their freedom when we've fully discovered it for ourselves.

Have you ever felt as if you are doing all the right things, yet the breakthrough you desire is still not taking place and time seems to be running out? Have you experienced seasons when, as much as you keep putting God first, you have not felt you are on the receiving end of God's miraculous breakthroughs at all? This can be the perfect platform for you to compare yourself negatively to others – but it doesn't have to be this way.

There's another Bible story of a righteous couple, faithfully serving the Lord but with a notable lack of one particular blessing – the gift of having a child. Luke describes Zechariah and Elizabeth as 'righteous in God's eyes, careful to obey all of the Lord's commandments and regulations' (Luke 1.6). Time was stacked against this couple in the natural course of things and they seemed unlikely ever to become parents.

Your breakthrough might not be in the area of pregnancy, but there is something in Elizabeth's story that can help you as you wait for your breakthrough and as you become a woman who champions other women in theirs. Whether you are holding out for breakthroughs in your workplace, in physical and mental health challenges, in relationships, in community engagement or another sphere and context, Elizabeth can show you something.

Elizabeth's husband Zechariah was a Jewish priest serving in the Temple. One day, while Zechariah was making his ritual sacrifice on behalf of the people, he came face to face with an angel. The angel announced that he and Elizabeth were going to have a baby boy, who would be called John.

True to promise, Elizabeth became pregnant. Like many women in her day she spent the majority of her pregnancy in relative seclusion, deeply aware of the kindness of the Lord. Even though Elizabeth had retreated from public life during her pregnancy she didn't become closed off to visitors. It was her openness to interruptions that the Angel Gabriel was just about to rely on! Some divine appointments only happen because we are willing to be interrupted; interruptions in our busy times as well as our restful times enable the Holy Spirit to usher in new purposes. Seasons of preparation can position us for divine directions. Wisdom will teach us the essential lesson of recognizing what is a Holy Spirit interruption and what is simply a distraction. Elizabeth was being prepared for a divine interruption.

Just over 80 miles away from Elizabeth, her cousin Mary was also visited by an angel with another announcement of a baby – Jesus. By means of encouraging Mary to believe in the inconceivable, the Angel Gabriel told her about Elizabeth, saying, 'What's more, your relative Elizabeth has become pregnant in her old age! People used to say she was barren, but she has conceived a son and is now in her sixth month. For nothing is impossible with God' (Luke 1.36–37). Heaven knew that the story of another woman's miraculous 'impossibility' had the potential to increase Mary's faith to receive the 'impossible' for herself.

Even though Mary had met an angel and felt the Holy Spirit overshadow her, she still needed to get herself into the company of another who would champion and encourage her: a woman who would recognize a miracle when she saw it, a woman who would not judge her but would witness to Jesus within her (literally) and support her unconditionally. Even though Mary was carrying Jesus she still needed to be in the company of a woman who would remind her of that truth! There were some tough days ahead for Mary and strength could be lost or gained depending on who she chose to connect with. Such is the significance of the courage that can be received when we champion one another.

In an interview with the BBC, Scottish psychologist Dr Kirsty Miller advocated the significant benefits women can experience when connecting with their friends, in terms of both physical and mental health as well as emotional well-being. Choosing and investing in the right friendships is good for us! 'Having people you enjoy spending time with can improve all aspects of our mental health,' explained Dr Miller. Getting together with friends can improve self-esteem while reducing depression, anxiety and stress. And it's not just our mental health that benefits when we spend time with friends: our physical health gets a boost too. 'When you're out with the girls and you're having a laugh, you feel a sense of release. There's the release of all these feel-good hormones; all the endorphins. It's a psychological burden being lifted.' And Dr Miller believes that turning down those invitations and neglecting our friends leaves us vulnerable. 'In terms of mental health you're more prone to depression,' she said. 'In older people it can lead to cognitive decline; basically your mental faculties slowing down.'[1]

You will have probably heard the expression that 'a problem shared is a problem halved' – well, consider how talking to someone of 'God-possibilities' can see faith shared and faith doubled!

Mary and Elizabeth's faith multiplied as they spent time with each other.

Mary is the only woman to carry the baby Jesus in her womb; however, all of us can carry his Spirit within us. As we do so, we would be wise to follow Mary's example and surround ourselves with those who will champion us and believe in who, or what, we are carrying.

Who, in your world, are the people who are living whole-heartedly for God first and have experienced that 'nothing is impossible with God'? They are the ones who will have the faith to encourage you when you are carrying something that seems impossible!

Luke tells the story:

A few days later Mary hurried to the hill country of Judea, to the town where Zechariah lived. She entered the house and greeted Elizabeth. At the sound of Mary's greeting, Elizabeth's child leaped within her, and Elizabeth was filled with the Holy Spirit.

Elizabeth gave a glad cry and exclaimed to Mary, 'God has blessed you above all women, and your child is blessed. Why am I so honoured, that the mother of my Lord should visit me? When I heard your greeting, the baby in my womb jumped for joy. You are blessed because you believed that the Lord would do what he said.'
(Luke 1.39–45)

Have you ever received a wonderful gift, bought yourself a fantastic outfit, written the best report, given the most amazing presentation, been on the most glorious of holidays – only to have someone come along who has just received an even more wonderful gift, bought an even more fantastic outfit (with the perfect colour and at half the price you paid), written a report more widely received and recognized, nailed their presentation and even received a standing ovation, promotion and pay rise, or has come back from an even better holiday with an even better tan? Have you ever felt as if your great experience has suddenly been dwarfed by someone trumping you with something better? As if the edge of your pleasure has been dampened? Has your good news ever felt deflated by the presence of someone else with even greater news?

Elizabeth has waited for years to become a mother and had all but given up. She is so blessed to become pregnant but the baby she is carrying is a signpost to another! He is a messenger. Elizabeth has every reason to celebrate, but then along comes Mary. Elizabeth's baby is a signpost for Mary's baby. Elizabeth carries the messenger whereas Mary carries the Message.

Elizabeth's response was beautiful and generous. Her years spent in the presence of God had prepared her to keep her gratitude and grace extended to this young, unmarried woman. All that was within Elizabeth leaped in delight and blessing for all that was within Mary. The huge significance of who Elizabeth carried was not dented by who Mary carried. What's more, Elizabeth saw beyond the scandal of the day to recognize that the Lord was ushering in divine purposes.

Elizabeth poured out encouragement, honour and blessing to Mary because she had plenty to give.

Now you might feel I'm being harsh – as if Elizabeth would begrudge Mary! As if any of us would ever begrudge another woman any blessing more than we have! As if! But to keep this real – I have seen so many women who are mightily blessed suddenly become jealous when they realize someone else seems *more* blessed! I've seen women who have waited so long for their breakthroughs becoming jealous when another woman seems to have been fast-tracked, women who have had so many challenges to endure in life becoming embittered towards someone who seems to have had an easy life with undeserved blessings.

When we allow the work of the Holy Spirit to fill us and to move, then we are able to sense the Spirit leaping within us to celebrate with other women. Even if others carry greater blessing, greater responsibilities, greater burdens, greater privilege, we can come alongside – encourage, honour and bless.

We, like Elizabeth, should never feel *less than* because of anyone else's *more than*! Comparison will lead us to feel *less than* because of someone's *more than*, but the Holy Spirit will reveal that our completeness in Christ is more than enough. The Holy Spirit within us will leap in delight when the Holy Spirit blesses another.

Elizabeth blessed Mary with the truth that 'you are blessed because you believed that the Lord would do what he said' (Luke 1.45). So too was Elizabeth. So too will we be.

Have you ever struggled to believe that you will be able to do something that the Lord has asked you to do? Recently I felt completely inadequate to do something that I felt the Lord had given me. The task seemed so great and I felt so small! As I wrestled with what I believed the Lord had asked me to do I began to feel isolated – as if nobody else understood. I wasn't able to explain clearly what I was experiencing but I knew the Lord was allowing me to experience a burden for the sake of some other people's breakthroughs, as well as my own. As I struggled I was suddenly reminded of a dear friend of mine. Anne has a mature prophetic gift. She champions many others and over the years has been a huge encouragement to me too. In my struggle the Lord was reminding me that I was not alone – of course he was with me, but there was a friend who would be too. As prophetic as Anne is, she is not a mind-reader and she is also juggling loads of different responsibilities. I could have said to the Lord that if he wanted me to chat with her then she should sense this and give me a call. I could have sat back and waited for the Lord to bring her to me. But just as Mary needed to head to the hill country, I needed to be willing to pick up the phone! For me to reach up to the Lord required me to reach out to others, and on this occasion I reached out to Anne. The Holy Spirit leapt within her as we chatted, and she encouraged me to grow in confidence that I had heard the Lord right, that what I was burdened with was from him. Because I reached out I was encouraged to press on.

A beautiful thing about the body of Christ is that it extends beyond location and denomination. So while there is a body locally to connect with, there is also a body internationally too! If you are a Mary then I assure you there are Elizabeths who are prepared, positioned and able to encourage and champion you. If you are an Elizabeth then there are Marys who need to interrupt you, be encouraged and mentored by you.

In my experience I am both a Mary to some and an Elizabeth to others! What we carry of the Holy Spirit can be encouraged by others who have gone before us but all of us, however young, can encourage others who are yet to have experienced what we have gone through.

I was connecting with my friend Emma recently. She is an airline pilot and a trailblazer for women in that role, who now encourages other women to aim high and train to be a pilot. When I asked about how she encourages women she amazed me by reminding me of the part that I played in her becoming a pilot – something I would never have taken any credit for! Several years ago she had failed her first command exams, and she reminded me that I championed her to keep going and try again. 'You told me it would refine me rather than define me and you were right.' What an encouragement that was to me to hear. Let's encourage each other to be *refined* and not *defined* by failures and to persevere for the purposes of the Lord to be realized in our lives. As a pilot mentor, Emma told me she has 'coached people through initial interviews and kept in touch with them through their training and in the early part of their careers. I hope I will still be part of their careers as they continue long after I hang up my flying boots.' Championing other women can last a lifetime.

One of my daughters recently sat some major exams and in the process of her studies spent time with an older 'Elizabeth' to help her study. She is a couple of years older than my daughter and had previously studied my daughter's course, so they arranged to meet in their lunch breaks to encourage my daughter to press on through the tricky stuff. What a pleasure it has been to observe this precious friendship between the girls. But my heart was so blessed recently when my daughter told me that she was looking out for some girls in the year below her at school – ready to pass on all her revision notes as soon as she had finished. However young or old you are, there are women positioned to encourage you, and you can position yourself to champion others.

Let's share and halve our problems and also share and multiply our faith!

23

What's yours is mine

There's a phrase linked to generosity that encourages us to say, 'What's *mine* is yours.' It is a give-away attitude that chooses generosity as a lifestyle. When it comes to discovering the freedom of championing other women, though, I've come to see that 'What's *yours* is mine' is even more important! It's not because we're grabbing something from someone – rather, we are celebrating. To understand this further we're going to take a look at the unlikely story of a mother and her daughter-in-law.

Defying all the jokes about mothers-in-law, the relationship between Ruth and her mother-in-law Naomi is exquisite.

Ruth's story joins her to the genealogy that will in time include Jesus. Just like the story of Leah and Rachel, Ruth and Naomi's story has been recorded to reveal something of the Father's love and character to us. However, there are some significant differences between the relationships of Leah and Rachel and Ruth and Naomi. These differences will give us keys to our freedom to conquer comparison as we move into liberty, away from the trap of jealousy.

A severe famine in Bethlehem meant Naomi, with her husband and two sons, had moved away to the more prosperous kingdom of Moab. They settled there and both sons married Moabite women. Tragically Naomi's husband and both sons died, leaving Naomi and her daughters-in-law Ruth and Orpah bereft of hope. Naomi decided to return to Bethlehem, but on the way back there the situation overwhelmed her and she realized she had nothing to offer her daughters-in-law. So out of her hopelessness she released the young women from their relational obligation to be with her, encouraging them to go back to their homeland of Moab, and Orpah reluctantly did so. So much grief engulfed these women as they hugged goodbye.

It is possible for relationships to end and go in different directions without animosity, but rather to pursue different purposes. I wish someone had told me at school that not all friendships would last a lifetime. We so often place expectations on friendships lasting for ever, but the reality is that when seasons, locations or occupations change, so can friendships. It doesn't need to mean fallouts and heartache. It doesn't mean the relationships are necessarily broken. But distance can creep in and relationships get redefined.

Orpah did not keep going in the same direction as Ruth and Naomi, and so the women made a break from each other with no apparent animosity. Learning to let go of some relationships when seasons change, with no hostility or division, is essential to enabling us all to pursue the purposes of the Lord. When seasons and friendships change, it doesn't need to be defined as failure, unfriending or becoming enemies but rather moving in a new direction.

Ruth, however, clung to her mother-in-law and refused to be redirected. She had become part of this woman's family through her marriage. She had lived as a member of this family for so many years and had adopted their values, their faith and their God. Her heart was so entwined that she was not going to let go! Perhaps her grief was so intense and flooded back over her, memories of her father-in-law, her brother-in-law and now her husband – all gone. Threefold grief would have gripped her heart and pulled her security and her happiness far from her, such that the thought of losing her mother-in-law too was simply unbearable.

Ruth's refusal to be broken from her betrothed family bond extended to her faith bond. Naomi's life of witness had impacted Ruth to such a degree that she was making faith steps of her own as she uttered, 'What's yours is mine,' to her mother-in-law, beseeching,

'Don't ask me to leave you and turn back. Wherever you go, I will go; wherever you live, I will live. Your people will be my people, and your God will be my God. Wherever you die, I will die, and there I will be buried. May the LORD punish me severely if I allow anything but death to separate us!' When Naomi saw that Ruth was determined to go with her, she said nothing more.
(Ruth 1.16–18)

Ruth aligned herself with the place, people and purpose of Naomi in a remarkable act of loyalty. She did not prioritize her own gain. Rather, she determined to invest her life in serving another woman's vision. This is a remarkable example which is still a challenge to us now. In a culture where we are encouraged to follow our dreams and reach our own potential, could we be as bold as Ruth to champion another woman?

Naomi had run out of arguments; there was no fight left in her. She was grateful for the company and loyalty as the two desolate women made their journey. The sadness and depression were so immense for the grieving Naomi that even on arrival, when warmly greeted by the women she used to spend her life with, her agony was apparent. She asked to be called Naomi no longer but instead to be called Mara – which means 'bitter'. Naomi knew herself through the pain and loss and reckoned everyone else might as well simply accept that this was who she had become. Even with Ruth's company she was living life on empty.

Ruth's reputation, on the other hand, was spreading via word of mouth around the town. Remember how we considered that our gifts do not need titles but rather will find their own space? Just so, Ruth's loyalty and generosity was becoming known, to the extent that a wealthy landowner called Boaz, a distant relative of Naomi's late husband, came to hear of her. When she found herself scavenging for scraps in Boaz's fields he spoke a blessing over her, saying,

But I also know about everything you have done for your mother-in-law since the death of your husband. I have heard how you left your father and mother and your own land to live here among complete strangers. May the LORD, the God of Israel, under whose wings you have come to take refuge, reward you fully for what you have done.
(Ruth 2.11–12)

In spite of the trauma of loss and the challenge of their circumstances, there was a blessing for Ruth that expresses the Lord's desire to be her safe place, her refuge. He wants to be the still place even in storms, the calm voice in all the chaos, the peace in all the noise and the protector even in our vulnerability.

As the book of Ruth continues, we see the hardworking humility of Ruth, the tenacity of Naomi and the grace of Boaz all entwining in a story of redemption and restoration. Ruth and Boaz end up marrying and the two women's circumstances are revolutionized. And as God changes the narrative of their futures, there is another opportunity for us to see the significance of a relationship between women who choose to celebrate one another's success and to champion one another.

Even though Ruth's life had become bitter she never allowed *herself* to become bitter. While life was really hard for Ruth she never allowed *herself* to become hardhearted.

Ruth and Boaz had a baby boy called Obed. This young boy would one day be grandfather to King David and part of Jesus' genealogical line. Obed is not just seen as the son to Ruth and Boaz, though, for

The women of the town said to Naomi, 'Praise the LORD, who has now provided a redeemer for your family! May this child be famous in Israel. May he restore your youth and care for you in your old age. For he is the son of your daughter-in-law

who loves you and has been better to you than seven sons!'
Naomi took the baby and cuddled him to her breast. And she
cared for him as if he were her own. The neighbour women
said, 'Now at last Naomi has a son again!' And they named
him Obed. He became the father of Jesse and the grandfather
of David.
(Ruth 4.14–17)

While he was not from her own womb, the child of Ruth was celebrated as if he were Naomi's. Naomi didn't become a baby-stealer,
she became a baby-celebrator! Ruth's happiness was enough for
Naomi to know happiness. Naomi's life turned from bitter to better,
not because of a blessing she directly or personally received, but
because of the blessing received by Ruth.

These two women had grasped a new freedom because they jour-
neyed through loss to a place of transformation where they truly
believed 'What's yours is mine.'

Would it have been possible for Rachel to be content with being
loved and to celebrate the fruitfulness of her sister Leah's womb
instead of her own, saying, 'What's yours is mine'? This is not to say
she would take any child from her sister but that she would celebrate
as if she had been directly blessed herself. Could one sister embrace
the success of the other as if her own – celebrating and championing
rather than competing with her?

As mentioned earlier in this book, when I was in a season of secondary infertility it was as if every woman around me was pregnant.
I'm not proud of my response to allow jealousy to grow within my
heart, as this allowed me to be robbed of sharing some joys that
other women were experiencing. It seemed a particularly fertile
time in the church and there were many Sundays when we were able
to dedicate young babies. There was a time when one of our elders
came alongside me at the end of the service and challenged me to
not simply 'smile and wave' in offering a surface-level celebration

for these families. Instead, she urged me to go deeper and *really* celebrate their seasons – even if such a blessing was never going to be mine directly! Not just pretending but really celebrating! Could their fertility be celebrated with as much joy as if it was mine? Could I celebrate from a deeper, more honest and authentic place alongside them?

Can you celebrate with *her* when *she* gets the audition call-back, or with *her* when *she* gets the promotion in your office? Can you celebrate with *her* when *she* gets the invitation, the date, the baby or the new car?

To celebrate with another is to love someone as yourself, which, as we've seen, can only really happen in all its fullness when we first love the Lord wholeheartedly. When with another woman we celebrate any favour or success she is enjoying, we are releasing our 'right' to have what she has. As we release our hold on our personal 'rights', we can choose to trust that our Heavenly Father has good plans for us too. Even if the Lord's plans for our life are completely different from the plans he has for *her*, they are still good – because *he is good.*

Naomi might not have been in a season when life was good, yet she knew that the Lord was good. She could trust him even when life was something to endure. Naomi was able to celebrate the favour that was being bestowed, not by vicariously living through Ruth, but rather by championing her from alongside. Vicarious living is living in the imagination through the actions of another person. Naomi was not imagining living well – she was actually living well when she saw the favour and restoration coming to Ruth. She didn't pretend to celebrate but rather really celebrated. She didn't pretend to champion her but really championed her. She didn't merely cheer Ruth on with her voice but cheered her on from her heart.

Comparison was conquered and Naomi's life went from bitter to better, not because of anything she herself directly received but because of what Ruth received. How would your life be better if you let go of any bitterness and championed another woman's success?

Instead of focusing on the lack of women who have made it through the 'glass ceiling', let's celebrate the ones that have. Instead of bemoaning the lack of women in a specific sphere, let's celebrate the ones that *are* there.

Ruth had not determined to follow a distant person – as we might on Instagram. She was not aligning with the idea of a person or an image of a celebrity. Ruth gave her loyalty and support to a woman who was broken, worn out by life, and who could provide nothing in return. She did not follow for the hope of reward or opportunity. She did not line up for the guarantee of what she could get out of the relationship. She and Naomi were heading towards an unknown people and an unknown place, as far as Ruth was concerned. The only familiarity known in Ruth's 'What's yours is mine' declaration was Naomi and God! The God that Naomi worshipped in Bethlehem was the same in Moab and would be the same when they came back to Bethlehem.

We will discover the freedom to champion other women when we are more interested in what we can give by means of support than in what we can receive in the form of opportunities, favours or 'likes'.

My friend Maria Rodrigues, who hosts Premier Radio's weekday *Woman to Woman* show, posted these encouraging words on Facebook:

There are around 3.5 billion women on this planet, each one with different hopes, dreams, fears and experiences. Some have doctorates, others are illiterate. Some have homes, others do not. Some love who they are, others can't stand themselves. Some feel inadequate, others are confident. If we grasp the reality that each one of us is unique and has a special contribution to make to this world then perhaps we would begin to realise what treasures we are and appreciate more deeply that there is no need to compare our lives or achievements with that of others. No-one else in the past, present or future will be exactly like you . . . you are an amazing one-off! Am celebrating who you are today.

It is time for us to become women who will allow the celebrations to begin between us and to practise growing in learning to love, free to celebrate and say, 'What's *yours* is mine.'

24

Let's do this!

As I draw this book to a close, I'm so mindful of the journey we've been on – and the open horizon ahead of us. As we've looked at stories of other women and their relationships, there's a challenge for our relationships, too. Let's take a quick moment to refresh our memories.

In Part 1 we looked at the battles that are close to home – uncomfortable scenes of sisters warring and the awareness growing that relationships between women matter, not just to us but possibly, like Euodia and Syntyche, to the whole Church and community.

Then there's the tendency to be like Martha, cooking up resentment by over-committing and then regretting it, and indirectly trying to heap guilt on to Mary so that she would get involved. But Martha was met by the loving grace of Jesus, who wouldn't let her manipulate anyone but instead encouraged her to reprioritize her own values. We don't know if Martha ever finished cooking the meal or if she joined her sister at Jesus' feet. What we do know is that, sometime later, when her brother died and was buried, she was the first of the sisters to leave her posture of grief and run to Jesus.[1] She knew where her hope and help came from and lovingly reminded her sister of this truth, urging her to leave her grief and draw close again to Jesus.

Let's learn the lesson from Rachel and not give our lives up to the pursuit of satisfying jealousy for what someone else has, when Christ gave his life up so that we have a way out from every temptation. We can conquer comparison because he has conquered sin.

In Part 2 we looked at how the relationships with other women in our places of work can sometimes be challenging. The heartache carried by Sarai became hardness in response to the contempt that Hagar felt towards her. Yet Hagar encountered the Lord and everything changed. When we know that we are seen and heard by God, doesn't everything change?

All of us have been given spiritual armour to put on each day before we put on anything else – armour that can change our relationships and help us truly conquer comparison.

In Part 3 we looked more deeply at some of our inner battles. We've seen the narrative that surrounds us, but sometimes the conversation of comparison is contained within us. I confess that when I wrote about impostor syndrome and that inner voice that chips away at women's confidence, I again had to remind myself not to fall prey to the lying voice. Escaping the comparison trap is not an abstract theory someone else may possibly experience, but a glorious opportunity of grace where you can walk free as yourself. You needn't remain chained with jealousy, in the claws of who you're not. This is a new way of living, where women like you and me will thrive in lasting liberation.

Remember the story of the tenacious and feisty pirate Gráinne Ní Mháille, who wielded her sword in the face of enemy attack even with her newborn baby on her hip? I'm not advocating a life of thieving at sea, but rather that we would be women who recognize enemy attacks and come out fighting – with the armour provided by the Lord.

Let's not forget Hannah and the internal transformation that took place long before her circumstances changed, because she found her new grace as she worshipped. Perhaps we will conquer comparison most effectively when we wield our swords from the position of kneeling in worship.

In Part 4 we looked at what it is to be body perfect. I don't mean in fitting into the most perfectly sculpted jeans but being a beautiful part of the body of Christ. I am a body part and so are you! We need each other. We need the women around us to function and thrive, uniquely gifted and uniquely placed. Together we can help any relationship ruptures (remember my Achilles!) to heal.

We are not called to compensate for the omissions of others but to make space, to participate actively, to use our gifts – practice will make our body perfect! Let's dance on Daddy's toes and enjoy it.

Finally, in Part 5 we explored what it might look like for us to champion other women instead of competing with them, to celebrate each other rather than comparing and becoming jealous. We are called to be she-witnesses – to say what we see Jesus doing and to speak what we've heard him say. We are not called to be judges.

We are all learners when it comes to loving others through life, but we have a great teacher in the Holy Spirit and plenty of opportunities to practise.

Ruth and Naomi discovered something so powerful when they said, 'What's yours is mine!' Who can you say those words to?

Before my sabbatical in the spring of 2019 I handed some batons to leaders on our team who were going to run with them on the next few laps of the race. As I write now, I am prayerfully imagining handing a baton to you. It is time we changed the narrative surrounding ourselves and all women. It is time to show the world what it really means for Christ to have come to set us free.[2] To live in the truth and the hope that we belong, we are positioned for purpose.

It's sometimes said that 'ignorance is bliss'. On the contrary, most would agree that often ignorance is dangerous. However, the reason it might be said to be bliss is because ignorance can imply a lack of responsibility. If we don't know about something then we don't need to do anything about it.

Well, we've gone on a journey together and as a result we cannot claim that we have no responsibility any more! We cannot claim ignorance because we've considered our relationships and those of other women. There is a battle raging around us that sees a very real enemy holding particular animosity against women and their offspring. That affects all of us! We are not each other's enemies. Together we can conquer the enemy who seeks to minimize us by restricting us to comparison – an enemy who loves it when we enter the 'sport' of putting women on pedestals and then knocking them off, an enemy who loves it when we compare and become jealous or when we project our own 'stuff' on to other unsuspecting women.

But enough attention to our enemy – the concluding words must all be from the heart of our Heavenly Father.

The truth that David grasped when he penned Psalm 139 is a truth just as relevant for you. Each one of us was seen in the unseen place of our mother's womb, crafted into the wonderfully complex women that we are, watched, as we were woven together, with the destiny of our days sketched out, super-loaded with potential. The Lord has innumerable thoughts towards each one of us and all of these thoughts are precious, to be treasured. He wants to surround us with the greatest force for good that we can experience.

Where you are right now, you are seen. Whether you are in what feels like a wilderness or enjoying life at an oasis, you are seen. You are known – you might wish you could hide some things but even the deepest of your thoughts are known. You are loved – strengths, weaknesses, passions, physically, mentally, emotionally – the whole of you is wholly loved. This wonderful truth is something that is applicable for all of us. This truth can make a difference to how you relate with all the women in your world.

The spectrum of womanhood is huge and God's love spans us all. Whether we 'click' with everyone or not has no effect on Christ's capacity or reach. Now, God can reach people in a supernatural, 'bright light' moment as women journey through their lives. However, the majority of times he chooses to express his love for others through us. When we work at *whatever* we do, for *whoever* our boss is, as if for the Lord, people can see him in us. His love can reach others through us.

Now is the time to grow in our capacity – to increase Christ's reach through us. The more we practise, the stronger his reach will become through us.

Let's look at the encouragement Paul gives,

> Bless those who persecute you. Don't curse them; pray that God will bless them. Be happy with those who are happy, and weep with those who weep. Live in harmony with each other. Don't be too proud to enjoy the company of ordinary people. And don't think you know it all!
>
> Never pay back evil with more evil. Do things in such a way that everyone can see you are honourable. Do all that you can to live in peace with everyone.
>
> Dear friends, never take revenge. Leave that to the righteous anger of God. For the Scriptures say,
>> 'I will take revenge;
>>> I will pay them back,'
>> says the Lord.
> Instead,
>> 'If your enemies are hungry, feed them.
>>> If they are thirsty, give them something to drink.
>> In doing this, you will heap
>>> burning coals of shame on their heads.'
> Don't let evil conquer you, but conquer evil by doing good. (Romans 12.14–21)

In our relationship with other women it's possible that we might feel as though someone is persecuting us when in fact she is doing nothing of the kind – remember the conversation I had with a lady on her deathbed. It is also possible that we might feel the persecution of another as Sarai felt the contempt of Hagar, or later how Hagar endured the harshness of Sarai. Whatever the circumstances, Paul's advice remains: pray for those you feel are persecuting you. Pray. Don't curse them, mutter under your breath or spread gossip about them. Pray blessing upon them. Pray that God's goodness is experienced by them.

Comparison and jealousy are conquered when we are happy with those who are happy and sad with those who are sad. It is the way we demonstrate 'What's yours is mine.' It is the way we don't just pretend to love but really love one another.

Don't let jealousy conquer you. It's time we conquered jealousy.

As we love the Lord wholeheartedly and completely, we can accept and receive his love in such a way that we can then give it away to others. This is how we love God first, then our neighbours and ourselves.

Let's join together and decide today that the narrative is being changed – one conversation, one thought at a time.

Together, we can conquer comparison and champion one another to a new destiny.

Let's practise gratitude and live as his witness. Let's practise forgiveness, letting go of the right to retain the pain and instead tearing up the record of wrongs. Let's pick up our phones and reach out to friends. Let's rebuild burned bridges and then walk over them. Let's live to express Christ's love rather than to impress an audience. Let's live to express his love, not to gain more 'likes'. Let's reach out because he's reached down. Let's keep our spiritual armour on and recognize who our enemy really is. Let's be those who search for the good, confident that we will find favour.[3]

Let's seize the moment and be women who really are liberated. Let's walk in the truth that sets us all free and finally conquer comparison, together.

Now a blessing for you and every woman in your world:

God bless you and keep you,
God smile on you and gift you,
God look you full in the face
     and make you prosper.
(Numbers 6.24–26, *The Message*)

Notes

1 What kind of woman?

1 Emily V. Gordon, 'Why women compete with each other', *The New York Times*, 31 October 2015.

2 Gordon, 'Why women compete with each other'.

3 <www.bbc.co.uk/news/world-africa-48120228>

4 <https://scroll.in/video/922916/watch-old-nike-advertisement-resurfaces-in-the-light-of-the-controversy-involving-caster-semenya>

5 <www.bbc.co.uk/sport/48340080>

2 The narrative

1 <www.sciencedaily.com/releases/2018/05/180509162653.htm>

2 Michelle Obama, *Becoming* (New York, Viking, 2018), p. 241.

3 Lindy Woodhead, *War Paint* (London, Weidenfeld & Nicolson, 2017), p. 17.

4 Woodhead, *War Paint*, p. 252.

5 Woodhead, *War Paint*, p. 435.

6 <www.stuff.co.nz/life-style/life/110650816/what-is-really-driving-the-vilification-of-meghan-markle>

7 <ca.hellomagazine.com/healthandbeauty/health-and-fitness/2019021167679/sarah-ferguson-online-bullying-hello-to-kindness-exclusive/>

3 Sisters at war

1 Liora Ravid, *Daily Life in Biblical Times* (GEFEN Publishing House, Jerusalem, 2013), pp. 173–4.

2 Ravid, *Daily Life in Biblical Times*, p. 175.

4 Cooking up resentment

1 Brené Brown, *The Call to Courage* (Netflix, 2019).
2 <https://drleaf.com/blog/how-to-deal-with-performance-anxiety-tips-to-overcoming-mental-blocks/>
3 <www.psycom.net/negativity-bias>

5 Contagion

1 Acts 15.39.

6 Conspiracy

1 Nicholas D. Kristof and Sheryl WuDunn, *Half the Sky: How to change the world* (Virago, London, 2010), p. xviii.
2 Kristof and WuDunn, *Half the Sky*, p. xix.
3 Kristof and WuDunn, *Half the Sky*, p. xix.

7 Work at *whatever*

1 <www.payscale.com/career-news/2018/10/heres-how-many-years-youll-spend-work-in-your-lifetime>
2 <www.bbc.co.uk/news/business-47934513>
3 Ephesians 6.5–9.
4 Mark Greene, *Fruitfulness on the Frontline* (Downer's Grove, Illinois, IVP Publishing, 2013), p. 18.
5 Greene, *Fruitfulness on the Frontline*, p. 160.
6 <https://fairygodboss.com/articles/female-rivalry-in-the-workplace-and-what-to-do-about-it>
7 <www.theatlantic.com/magazine/archive/2017/09/the-queen-bee-in-the-corner-office/534213/>
8 <www.theatlantic.com/magazine/archive/2017/09/the-queen-bee-in-the-corner-office/534213/>

8 You are seen

1 Priscilla Shirer, *The Resolution for Women* (Nashville, Tennessee, B & H Publishing Group, 2011), p. 256.

2 <www.learnreligions.com/what-is-midrash-2076342>

3 <www.chabad.org/library/article_cdo/aid/112053/jewish/Hagar.
htm>

4 Genesis 18.12.

9 Holiness, not holey-ness

1 Genesis 17.15–16.

10 Wear the uniform

1 <www.bbc.co.uk/news/uk-england-london-36264229>

2 <www.bbc.co.uk/news/uk-3966791>

3 Ephesians 4.14.

4 John 20.5.

11 Do you belong here?

1 Michelle Obama, *Becoming* (New York, Viking, 2018), p. 56.

2 Matthew 9.20–22; Mark 5.25–34; Luke 8.43–48.

3 Leviticus 15.19–33.

4 <www.therefinersfire.org/tallit.htm>

5 <www.therefinersfire.org/tallit.htm>

12 Hush

1 <www.tech21century.com/the-human-brain-is-loaded-daily-
with-34-gb-of-information/>

2 <www.theguardian.com/media/2005/nov/19/advertising.
marketingandpr>

3 <www.wordstream.com/blog/ws/2018/07/19/advertising-statistics>

4 <drleaf.com/about/toxic-thoughts/>

5 <drleaf.com/blog/5-mental-health-mistakes-that-could-be-
causing-you-unnecessary-anxiety/>

13 It's to be expected

1 Elizabeth Foley and Beth Coates, *What Would Boudicca Do?*

Everyday problems solved by history's most remarkable women (London, Faber & Faber, 2018), front cover.

2 Foley and Coates, *What Would Boudicca Do?*, p. 50.

3 Foley and Coates, *What Would Boudicca Do?*, p. 52.

4 Foley and Coates, *What Would Boudicca Do?*, p. 53.

5 <drleaf.com/blog/people-pleasing-how-it-can-damage-your-mental-health-and-how-to-stop/>

6 <drleaf.com/blog/people-pleasing-how-it-can-damage-your-mental-health-and-how-to-stop/>

14 A new grace

1 <www.behindthename.com/name/hannah>

2 Frank Damazio, *From Barrenness to Fruitfulness: How God can use you to birth new life in your church* (Raleigh, North Carolina, Regal House Publishing, 2001), pp. 121–2.

3 Acts 2.13.

4 John 20.7–8.

5 Damazio, *From Barrenness to Fruitfulness*, p. 137.

6 Damazio, *From Barrenness to Fruitfulness*, p. 141.

15 Hold on!

1 Lisa Bevere, *Without Rival: Embrace your identity and purpose in an age of confusion and comparison* (Ada, Mississippi, Revell Books, 2016), p. 89.

2 <drleaf.com/blog/why-failure-is-one-of-the-best-things-to-happen-to-us/>

16 Broken bodies

1 Genesis 1.26.

2 Genesis 2.18.

3 Galatians 4.6—7.3

4 Genesis 3.15.

17 Flawsome!

1 <www.churchofengland.org/prayer-and-worship/worship-texts-and-resources/common-worship/marriage>
2 Rachel Gardner, *The Girl De-Construction Project: Wildness, wonder and being a woman* (London, Hodder & Stoughton, 2018), p. 29.

18 Becoming you!

1 Proverbs 18.16.
2 <drleaf.com/blog/5-mental-health-mistakes-that-could-be-causing-you-unnecessary-anxiety/>
3 Beth Moore <@BethMooreLPM>, Twitter, 7 May 2019.
4 Michelle Obama, *Becoming* (New York, Viking, 2018), pp. 328, 333.

21 Wearing L-plates

1 Romans 12.9.
2 Conrad Gempf, *How to Like Paul Again: The apostle you never knew* (Milton Keynes, Authentic Publishing, 2013), p. 106.
3 R. T. Kendall, *The Anointing: Yesterday, today, tomorrow* (London, Hodder & Stoughton, 1998), pp. 189–90.
4 Kendall, *The Anointing*, p. 124.
5 Kendall, *The Anointing*, p. 199.

22 Let him leap!

1 <www.bbc.co.uk/programmes/articles/MmbBMkc916M8K2ZmQ1rycq/why-a-festive-night-out-with-friends-is-good-for-your-health>

24 Let's do this!

1 John 11.20.
2 John 8.31–32.
3 Proverbs 11.27.